I Love Everybody

(and Other Atrocious Lies)

ALSO BY LAURIE NOTARO

The Idiot Girls' Action-Adventure Club

Autobiography of a Fat Bride

I Love Everybody

(and Other Atrocious Lies)

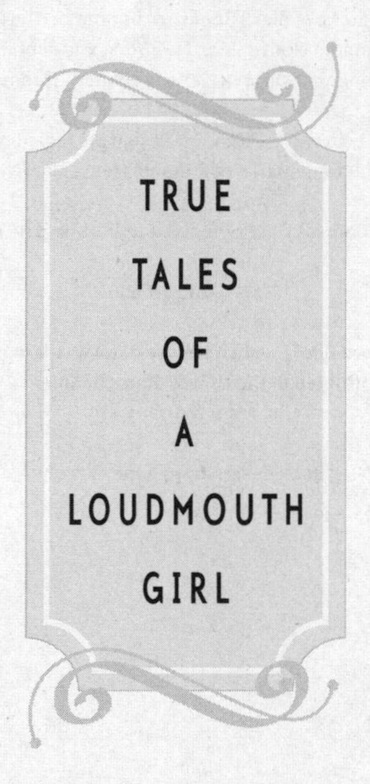

Laurie Notaro

VILLARD
NEW YORK

2004 Villard Books Trade Paperback Original

Published in the United States by Villard Books, an imprint of The Random House Publishing Group, a division of Random House, Inc., New York, and simultaneously in Canada by Random House of Canada Limited, Toronto.

VILLARD and "V" CIRCLED Design are registered trademarks of Random House, Inc.

Library of Congress Cataloging-in-Publication data is available.

ISBN 0–8129–6900–6

Villard Books website address: www.villard.com
Printed in the United States of America
2 4 6 8 9 7 5 3 1

Book design by Jo Anne Metsch

To D. O. Hopkins

and my Pop Pop:

Wish you were here.

Contents

I Love Everybody

(and Other Atrocious Lies)

Gun to the Head

"I can't believe it," my mother said from her end of the phone, "I simply can't believe it. First you got married, and now this. Who would have thought a year ago that I would be hearing news like this!"

"I know!" I exclaimed from my end of the phone. "I'll get to go shopping for new clothes and everything!"

"It's a big thing," my mother added. "It will change your whole life, you know."

"I know," I said happily. "But I think it's time. That clock was ticking, and it was just time I did something about it."

"You're sure this is what you want?" my mother asked.

"It's too late to turn back now, isn't it?" I laughed. "I took the test, got a little pee on my hand, and everything says we're good to go."

"I can't wait to tell my friends!" my mother gushed.

"Well, maybe that's not such a good idea just yet," I suggested. "Maybe we should see if it sticks first. But you can tell Dad and the rest of the family."

"He's going to be so happy to find out that you're going to have"—my mother paused, I believe to wipe a tear of elation from her eye—"a job!"

A job.

I really couldn't believe it either. A job. After I had successfully passed the drug screening test (simply and vaguely put, I was a freelance writer with a mortgage payment and a husband in college who barely had enough money for a generic box of macaroni and cheese, let alone a hit of X just so I could have a good excuse to wear a Dr. Seuss hat), the newspaper at which I had been a freelance columnist also offered me a job as a columnist for the newspaper's website—a full-time gig. I could hardly pass the offer up; it was a good salary, came with health insurance, my potential boss seemed cool, and after I discovered that the 401(k) was not an annual marathon that every employee was required to participate in, I nodded and then we shook on it.

In all honesty, it was a relief. The last time I had held a steady job it was as an editor for a small magazine several years before. I worked for a man who commonly came back from business lunches with a big purple wine mustache and had the habit of uttering phrases such as "make that more better," "irregardless," "for all intensive purposes," and picking a five-syllable word from the dictionary then e-mailing it out to the staff as the "word du jour of the day!" which for an average drunk boss would be fine, but for an editor in chief was somewhat unsettling.

After he called me into his office one day and slid two envelopes across the table—one for my last paycheck and the other for severance—he tried to soften the blow with the comforting words, "Don't look so upset! You're not being fired, your position has just been eliminated!" It wasn't a surprise per se, I had expected the Two Envelope Incident ever since I had freely used the phrase "blow your wad" in an editorial meeting when vocalizing an opinion about why it would be a mistake to name the murderer in the headline of an investigative piece about a longtime unsolved crime. From across the table, I had seen his purple mustache quiver, then collapse into a frown.

Matter of time.

Since then I had embarked on a series of freelance jobs that led me down the creative, soul-drenching path of writing about air conditioners with pollen-capturing filters; weaving prose about toenail fungus and the bacteria living happily in the track of your shower door that can kill at will; two hundred witty and classic-caliber-status product reviews of kitchen gadgets, including profiles of slotted spoons, rubber spoons, stainless steel spoons, serving spoons, and the good old spoon spatulas (spoonulas); a pamphlet about the money-saving benefits of hiring temps; and a booklet about gun safety.

Honestly, I didn't go to journalism school to write pamphlets advising otherwise oblivious parents that it would be in their best interest to store their loaded weapons out of reach of their young-uns, but one day I found myself in a job interview discussing just that.

With a gun in the middle of the table.

"Have you ever held a gun before?" the lady whom I was meeting with asked me.

"No, no," I said with a little nervous laugh, feeling a little under-qualified for the job. "My family were staunch believers in *physical* violence, not *automatic* violence, and we had a Safeway around the corner, so we never really needed to kill anything."

"Would you like to hold the gun?" the lady asked. "It would be useful to know what a gun looks like when writing the material for the booklet."

"Oh. Oh, okay, in that case," I replied nodding hesitantly, as I reached slowly for the gun.

"It's not loaded," the lady informed me with a wave of her hand.

"Sure, that's what they all say," I tried to joke, with a wave of *my* hand that wasn't touching a deadly weapon.

I picked it up. It was heavy. It was some sort of pistol, I don't know what kind, but I did know that I did NOT like having a gun so close to me. I felt like I should be wearing a tracksuit with racing stripes or a Members Only windbreaker and sucking on a tooth-pick.

"Okay, that's good," the lady said, then put her hand out. "I'll take it now."

So I handed her the gun, I mean, it was *her* gun, *I* certainly hadn't brought a gun to the meeting, what was I going to say, "No, Annie Oakley, you can't have your gun"?

What was I supposed to do?

Obviously, however, I had done the wrong thing. Because in a fraction of a moment, I was looking down the barrel of a gun that was now being pointed straight at me. At my head. It was nothing short of a miracle that I did not suddenly lay a big brown egg in my pantalones, if you know what I mean.

"NEVER," the lady commanded, "LET ANYONE TAKE A GUN AWAY FROM YOU, NEVER."

Holy shit, I thought. *Holy shit. Holy shit. Holy shit.* What the hell is happening here? What the hell just happened? Is the gun lady going to kill me? Did she lure me here to kill me? Oh my God, I'm not *that* Notaro! I wanted to scream. *Those people live in New Jersey!*

"IF YOU GIVE SOMEONE A GUN, THEY JUST MAY POINT IT AT YOU," she continued, the pistol still focused on the spot between my eyes.

"You said it wasn't loaded," I said, trying to stay calm.

"And you believed me?" the gun lady said. "I only met you five minutes ago."

I really didn't know what to do. Should I be putting my hands up at this point? I wanted to ask her; if it's possible, could you shoot me in a major organ below my neck as opposed to, say, an eye, I don't want to be the ghost with one eye or half a face or anything like that, I would prefer to be *spooky* in the spirit afterlife, not *creepy*; can you please dump my body where someone will find me relatively quickly so my mother can have the funeral she's always dreamed of because it will be hard for folks to work up an appetite for the party after if they know I'm all rotten and yucky under the lid, and I bet she'll probably have better catering at this shindig than she did at my wedding, so if I'm all decomposed it will *totally* ruin the whole thing for her; do I have time to make a phone call so I can tell someone what I want to be buried in, because otherwise, I'll be spending the remainder of history in my *Gone with the Wind* wedding dress, and it's superhard to pee in, a skirt would be much better, especially if the afterlife has a bar; and by the way, I am not having an affair with your husband, if that's what this is all about, and if you're having an affair with mine, he's all yours. Enjoy the ear hair, it keeps getting longer *every day*.

Instead, I just looked at her and decided I really didn't need to be concerned with being rude at this point, since lethal elements had already been introduced into the scenario, so I said, "You know, you are really freaking the shit out of me."

"That," she said as she smiled and put the gun back on the table, "was your first lesson in gun safety."

I just looked at her as my heart dropped to my ankles.

"I can pay you eight hundred dollars," she said. "Are you interested?"

Considering that I had a mortgage payment due, the aforementioned husband in college, and not enough disposable income to even entertain the thought of purchasing illicit drugs that I desperately needed at that very moment, I nodded.

"Sure," I said. "Why not. But if you need anything written about butcher-knife or machete safety, I'm not your girl."

With experiences like that one ringing the memory bell, I took the job at the newspaper and got ready to become employed. I got a Banana Republic credit card and charged away.

Having a job, I quickly found, involved more than orchestrating a visually delightful and stunning ensemble every day and then having the opportunity to show it off, especially when it's required that you absolutely ruin your fashion gift to the rest of the building with a big, huge, nasty plastic badge pinned to your brand-new, perfect, and as of yet unblemished white Banana Republic shirt purchased at full price.

Especially when the picture on that badge resembles one of the more unflattering photos of Janet Reno wearing the same full-price Banana Republic shirt although it is your name printed beneath it. And you are never, ever, *ever* granted an additional opportunity to take another badge photo unless you are disfigured in a gasoline/propane/diesel fuel accident, lose a nose, or have the vanity to cough up the twenty-dollar replacement-badge fee. Which I did not, since I already owed Banana Republic my first eight paychecks.

On my first day at my new job, I was thrilled to find out that I had a real office—not a cubicle, not a desk among many, but a real-live office with a door and a window and my own phone extension. Woodward and Bernstein never had it so grand, I thought, and as I sat down and wrote my first column as a full-time columnist, it felt pretty good.

I was really happy. I loved my job.

I had an hour for lunch, a wonderful editor, the office was close to my house, making my commute about seven minutes, and I now had health insurance for the first time in years. I reveled in the fact that if I now had a sore throat, I could actually go to the doctor instead of rummaging through my mother's medicine cabinets looking for expired antibiotics and hoping I hadn't grabbed her hot-flash hormone pills by mistake.

I was going to take full advantage of my new coverage too, despite the fact that I believe that I've been dead for a while. I am only able to wake up on a daily basis because the things keeping my body together are the preservatives and chemicals found in all Hostess products, chocolate-flavored Twizzlers, Bugles, and particularly Funyuns. Due to my snack-oriented eating habits, I believe I was completely embalmed by the time I graduated high school, and as a result, my molecules are most likely bound together in some sort of a plasticlike riboflavin substance. In several years when my shelf life expires, my edges will become hard, crusty, and kind of yellow, and you'll know I've passed when I simply stop talking or am no longer rolling my eyes at other people when they are speaking.

Nevertheless, in recent years, the parts of me that believed they were still alive tried to reinforce their philosophy by emitting sharp, stabbing pains and on occasion, spectacular thrusts of discomfort. I'm sure this has probably happened all my life, but now that I was swimming around in my thirties and people my age didn't really die from simple things like mixing Jim Beam and downers anymore but from causes that require more treatment than substance abuse programs, it brought those bolts of ache to the forefront. I started paying closer attention to these episodes, and mapped out the occurrences on a grimacing stick figure I drew named "Laurie's Random Pain Pangs." Oddly enough, most of the regions seemed to be located where there aren't organs or anything with a specific function, so I could at least then say, "Whoa, there goes my gallbladder and that tortilla chip I apparently didn't chew very well," or, "There's that aorta constricting again!" Nope. These places were basically empty spots, or places I thought were just used for storage, for things like extra bile, a couple of feet of rolled-up intestine, balls of hair that may come in handy in the future, maybe some additional vein parts, and bits of corn. Therefore, I had no other choice than to believe these pangs were cancer announcing its arrival, just to let me know it's moved in.

Knock, knock.

Who's there?

It's Cancer.

Cancer who?

Cancer of the Section Right Behind Your Belly Button That You Have Been Trying to Pass Off as the Pinch of Ovulation. But It's Not. It's Cancer. It's *Me.*

It wouldn't be at all surprising. In my family, you have just as good of a genetic chance that you will get cancer as you will get an eye. It's that built in. It comes with the package.

So far, according to my map, in addition to Cancer of the Section Right Behind My Belly Button That I Have Been Trying to Pass Off as the Pinch of Ovulation, I also had Cancer of the Place Below My Last Rib on the Left Side, Cancer of the Fatty, Puffy Spot Right Above My Right Knee, Thumb Cancer, and Cancer of the Upper Asshole.

Having health insurance was a definite plus, because not only did it look like cancer was going to call in all of my bets, but I was also convinced that every time I heard about a new, horrible affliction, I was positive it was my destiny to get it and I began exhibiting symptoms immediately. I was like the Zelig of disease. When my sister told me that her neighbor had some virus that disfigured her entire face with large, protruding lumps that could not be cured, I found several of my own in my neck, but thankfully my doctor informed me that they were my lymph nodes and it would be in my best interest to stop trying to pop them. After I read a story about fibromyalgia in *Ladies' Home Journal* in my mother's bathroom (limited availability of reading material; it was either that or my mom's favorite book, *Find Me* by Rosie O'Donnell), I started getting aches and pains all over my legs, until my doctor pointed out that my feet were stuffed into my shoes like pig's feet in a jar, and it didn't matter if the shoe on sale was not available in a seven and a half, only a six and a half, *I still had to buy my own size.* And when smallpox was mentioned as a possible biological weapon, I developed tiny bumps all over and thankfully my doctor looked me over and said, "You've been here three times in two weeks. I'm glad you have insurance, too, but there is nothing I can do for pimples. You have pimples, lymph nodes, and tight, cheap shoes. Go home, wash your face, and only call me from now on if you see blood."

Still, although my job gave me a host of things to celebrate, there were some drawbacks, too. I know that people are led to believe via television that the life of a columnist (e.g., Carrie Bradshaw) is a glamorous one filled with fancy clothes, fabulous parties, and Apple laptops.

That, I'm afraid, is a lie.

In the first place, no one at my newspaper looked like Sarah Jessica Parker, because if we had, we wouldn't be wasting our time at a newspaper, we'd have a series on HBO. Plus, to be blunt, you'd find a better-looking group of people working the overnight shift at Denny's than you would at a newspaper. It's no modeling agency, I'll tell you that much. Pick a random newsroom from anywhere across the country; they will all look like they just crawled out from Middle-earth. You see, in journalism school, the day comes when you have to make a choice: broadcast journalism or print journalism. The pretty people choose broadcast; the hominids choose print. If a hominid tries to stray over to the group in which she clearly doesn't belong, the pretty people will pelt her with expensive hair-care products, microphones, lip gloss, and call her fat until she rejoins her proper and rightful tribe. Likewise, if a pretty talking head tries to cross the line to the print group, we would have beat her with notepads, tape recorders, and keyboards and called her "Barbie" until it was time to eat her.

Now, even though I was with the correct group as far as my physical appeal was concerned, I had the feeling that I might not be the ideal fit for a corporate environment when I plopped my Pull My Finger Fred doll, my cow that pooped brown jelly beans, and my giant roll of butt floss on my desk for decoration, conversation icebreakers, and exciting indications of the jovial, frolicsome personality that bubbled like a spring underneath my new Banana Republic wardrobe. I thought people would get a kick out of them as much as I did (come on—cows pooping jelly beans! *brown jelly beans!*), but once I understood that my toys were displayed in the same area where other women my age (but looked much, much, *much* older and seemed very tired) had photos of their kids, their husbands, and either Xena the Warrior Princess or Ben Affleck, it also clearly explained the scary abundance of grown-ups in the lobby and on the elevator.

Now, the elevator posed some real problems for me, because since I worked on the seventh floor, I had a lot of time to examine people while riding in it. It clearly reinforced the fact that I was not corporate material. All of the people on the third floor, where the telemarketing/call center was located, looked as if they were bussed in from the methamphetamine part of town and spent their days off (when they weren't cooking up some supplemental income in their biohazard kitchen) having supervised visitation with their kids, who were now in some process of foster care or state custody; the folks on the fourth floor, specimens from the advertising and sales staff, had great tans, chemically altered white teeth, and boobs that started at their collarbones; the tenth-floor people, who held the keys to the kingdom below them, were a bunch of stern, unhappy VPs and execs who looked like they had mandatory rectal exams every morning before they were permitted to get into their Lexuses and go to work. They also had exquisite, beautiful bathrooms on their floor, so marvelous and resplendent they could have belonged to a dictator, which I felt free to use and enjoy as my own personal potty. It turns out that the elevator was a wonderful litmus test for exposing the true personalities of my coworkers as they revealed their inner selves in a thirty-six-square-foot compartment. One of them, a middle-aged woman who still really considered herself eye candy instead of an eyesore, never thought twice, when the elevator had a member of the opposite sex in it, about pulling up her skirt and exclaiming, "Oh, look at my legs! I've forgotten to put lotion on this morning! My skin is so dry! It's a good thing I keep lotion in my purse!" *Any* member of the opposite sex, including old men and children who were participants in Take Your Son to Work Day, whom she would obliviously shame as he nervously tried to keep his eyes focused on anything but her legs, which were so worn and broken-in that they could have easily been made into a Dooney & Bourke satchel. It was no surprise to me, then, when it was discovered she was messing around with her boss, who then left his wife and family for the purse with legs; he then bought her a truck, and two days after his divorce was final, she dropped him and her lotion bottle for a guy in IT.

The elevator granted me the opportunity not only to find out who the office sluts were; the nosybodies, the self-absorbed, the smelly, and the clueless all introduced themselves one by one on my flights seven stories up while they annoyed me in various other ways as well.

I hated them. It was an entirely new breed I hadn't encountered before.

They were the Elevator People. Now, honestly, I kept my hatred of the Elevator People to myself because I thought I was alone, it wasn't to be shared. Then, one day, I heard on the news about how a guy in Canada went berserk and unleashed a canister of pepper spray in an elevator when he had a fight with one of the other passengers about pushing excessive buttons.

I nodded and almost cried with relief when I heard the story. "Elevator People!" I whispered to myself. Finally, they had pushed someone too far. I knew exactly what he had been through, and this was a *Canadian*. Canadians are specially bred to be overtly nice, so you know what happened had to be bad. I knew exactly what kind of Elevator People were involved.

They were the people who got into the elevator after they had eaten pickled herring and raw onion for lunch and then insisted on laughing heartily when nothing funny had happened. The people who make the elevator experience an endurance test for the other elevator riders by holding the door open with a body part while feeling free to finish up the last fifteen minutes of a conversation. The people who go up or down only one floor.

As a matter of fact, my trip in the elevator most mornings was like a math problem straight out of the SATs. The question would read: "How long will it take Laurie to get to her desk if she and two men get on the elevator on the first floor, she pushes 8, the next man pushes 7, and the other man pushes 9, but on the second floor, a new man gets on and pushes 4, on the third floor, a lady gets on and pushes 5, on the fourth floor, the second-floor man gets out, on the fifth floor, the third-floor lady gets out but another one gets on and pushes 6, on the sixth floor, the fifth-floor lady gets out but another one wants on and hasn't decided where to meet her sixth-floor friend for lunch so she blocks the elevator door with her foot in a very scuffed-up Payless shoe and says, 'Downtown Deli? No, we ate there yesterday. Uno's? No, the wait is too long. Subway? No, I feel like something hot. Well, what are you in the mood for? Any ideas? No, I can't eat another hot dog after I got sick on that last one. Remember, it was all green at the end? Yuck. Hmmmm. I don't know. Well, just call me and we'll decide. Okay, I'll call you. Or you call me. Okay, I'll call you. Okay, sure, I'll call you. Hey, what about Chinese?' until the door wants to close so badly it threatens to slice her cheap little shoe right off her foot like it was deli ham, so she gets on and then naturally goes to push—what else—7, but the first-floor man already selected it, on the seventh floor the first-floor man gets off alone, and before the elevator hits eight, the Payless-shoe woman realizes she's missed the seventh floor and pushes 7 again? How long will it take before Laurie reaches her desk? What are the chances that she *will even survive?*"

Well, I'll tell you how long—it took me less time to drive to work than it did for me to get upstairs. So you see, I could completely understand how a gentle, nice-almost-to-the-point-of-being-retarded Canadian could unleash pepper spray in an elevator that eventually forced the evacuation of an entire building because every time the doors opened, the spray was spread. I could understand that. While I had never truly considered brandishing a weapon in the elevator, I had often thought about pinching people. Okay, that's a lie, I had often fantasized about a cattle prod, but only for the One Floorers. Only for them. And the Payless shoe lady, for her, too. I mean ONE FLOOR, I could never understand why people needed to take the elevator for ONE FLOOR. In my opinion, the company needed to send out a memo that said, "Hey, guess what, you guys! Ever wonder what's behind the mystery door? It's STAIRS! We have *STAIRS!* STAIRS are very similar to an escalator, but one that's MANUALLY OPERATED."

Because I'm telling you, after that day of the elevator math problem, if another person got on that elevator to travel eight feet upward, I couldn't have been responsible for what I did. I had been pushed to the limit. The next time it happens, I swore to myself, I'm going to reach out and pinch that One Floorer and say, "You get out there and *walk*! You won't come close to burning a fraction of the three thousand calories you ate at lunch, but maybe by the time you reach the landing, you'll pass out from exhaustion and get to go home for the rest of the day, you lazy little asshole, because that's exactly what you want anyway!"

I think it's fair to say I wasn't exactly fitting the corporate mold.

One day in the middle of spring, after our newspaper was bought by a large media conglomerate and new management took over, I was summoned to the office of the New Big Cheese for a "Hi, I'm Your New Boss" meeting. With my luck, it was during the week that my allergies had been the worst they had been all season—my nose was red, chafed, and peeling like a snake, my sinuses felt like someone had poured the foundation to a house into them, I had become a mouth breather, which is never a pretty look and for some scientifically undocumented reason makes allergy sufferers speak like a preschooler, substituting *b* for most letters, even some vowels. Worried that my column was on the chopping block, I popped a bunch of Claritin, slapped some moisturizer on my nose to reduce the skin flake shedding, got all dressed up, and tried to look presentable for the meeting. But when I walked into his office, I knew that even a makeover by Marcia Brady wasn't going to help me.

Once I saw the rectal expression on his face, I was concerned that someone may have reported me for engaging in a simulated pinching fantasy incident on the elevator or told him I had been running to the tenth-floor Saddam Hussein Palace bathroom clutching my abdomen an unnecessary number of times.

But he didn't say anything about that.

"Hi," he said.

"Hellob," I said back with a little wave.

"So, you're Laurie Notaro," he said, leaning back in his chair.

"Yeb," I said as I sat down. "Nice to beet youb."

He nodded.

I nodded back.

A snowflake of skin fluttered off my nose, drifting back and forth, twirling here and there, flutter, flutter, flutter, until it landed on his table.

"Do you like being a columnist?" he said, trying not to stare at me shedding.

"Yeb, berry much," I replied, then decided to make a joke. "I'b too ugly for teebee."

"That's good," he said, looking a little confused.

Now, at this point, the man's expression had remained so constant that I wasn't even sure he had teeth. I had a feeling he wasn't going to be joining my rotation list for lunch dates.

"We're making some changes to the section that your column appears in and—" He stopped short and focused his eyes on my nose.

And then I saw it. Granted, I didn't have the vantage point the New Big Cheese had—a full frontal view—but even I, looking down, could see something impressive taking place.

From above, I saw that it was shiny, spherical, and magnificent in size.

I, unbeknownst to even myself, had blown an incredibly large bubble from my right nostril, and it was the size of Biosphere 2.

It was enormous.

"Oh by Gob!" I cried suddenly, covering my nose with my hands as the Big Cheese looked at me, his mouth agape.

I saw that he did, indeed, have teeth.

"Oh by Gob!" I cried over again. I'm sure it was as disturbing to watch as it was to produce, but I had no idea of what I should do. So following my initial instinct (HIDE!), I scurried around but couldn't find any plants or furniture that I could throw myself behind, and I did that until I felt my second instinct (RUN!).

I ran around his office a couple more times as the new editor struggled to follow me, holding out something white and floppy—it could have been a tissue, for all I know, but the moment contained so many elements of a disaster that the white thing could have been a handkerchief, a sock, or his underwear, or it may have been a restraining order to keep me away from his office. Finally, I located his door during my last panic lap around the office, bolted out of it, and scurried down to my office and slammed my door shut.

I blew a mammoth orb out of my nose, I kept saying to myself. It must have looked like a comic strip; he was probably waiting for words to appear in it, saying something like, "*Esta burbuja del moco representa mi amor para usted, mi hombre lujurioso de la cara de rectal. ¡Pínchelo! ¡Pínchelo ahora!* (This snot bubble represents my love for you, my lusty rectal-face man. Pop it! Pop it now!)" I blew a bubble out my nose. A bubble, a big, nasty bubble, nearly the size of Christina Ricci's head, came right out of my face.

My column is history.

My column is so gone.

"OUT!" I was sure the Big Cheese was saying right at that moment, "Bubble Girl's column is out! Unless she's filling some special needs quota for the paper, she's out! Let her go get a job in the circus, where her kind belongs! Don't let her back in the building! God knows where else she may have bubble portals!"

I was going to lose my column because of the snot balloon, everyone was going to find out why, and I was going to have to quit in order to avoid all the embarrassing questions, whispers, stares.

I was going to have to quit. Well, I thought, trying to console myself, at least it's a first. You've never really been able to give notice before your employers have done it for you.

AND THAT, a big, deep, determined voice in my head suddenly interrupted the other voice in my head, IS WHY LAURIE NOTARO NEVER QUITS. SHE NEVER QUITS!! SHE IS NOT A QUITTER!! SHE'S A TWO-ENVELOPE GIRL!!

Hey, that's right, I said to myself, although I'm not sure in what voice; it was high and squeaky, so perhaps it was my inner Dr. Phil child voice. I love severance! I love it! I will not quit this job that I love. I will not walk away from it. I will swim through this snot-bubble muck!

I grabbed my chair, pulled it out, sat down in front of my computer and got ready to work, and that's when I suddenly sucked in a deep breath and gasped. I knew right then I couldn't quit anyway, even if I were blowing bubbles out both nostrils like a mermaid.

I found a pen, rifled through some papers, drew an arrow, and wrote the words "Cancer of the Lower Asshole" right next to the bottom half of my stick figure.

Baby No Name

With exactly six days to go before her due date, my pregnant sister Lisa sat on my Nana's couch and flipped through a baby name book.

"I don't know," she kept repeating over and over again. "I just don't know. I can't find anything I like."

Admittedly, she was cutting it close, but I'm not so sure that was really all her fault. Every Sunday around the dining room table, my family would try to help my sister find a good, strong name. The problem with that scenario, however, was the tendency of the members of my family—Italian Americans *from New York*—to believe that they each had found the perfect name and that everyone else's choice was a sin against nature.

It was a battle no one was winning, including my sister, and after what she had been through with this pregnancy, she should have at least qualified to be a leading contender.

A minute after Lisa learned she was pregnant with her second child, her belly expanded to the size of a room addition and salespeople began asking if she was expecting triplets. By now she hadn't crossed her legs in nearly a year, required a scouting expedition to navigate the widest path through restaurants, and couldn't get out of a car without the assistance of two Teamsters. Last week when we were at the mall, I looked at her and wondered how she was even able to stand upright, but at least I was happy that someone in my family had wider, more established stretch marks than I did.

Later that day, as we passed by a rack full of lingerie on sale, she looked longingly at lace demi-bras, the frilly underwires and padded little helpers. "Oh boy, I remember these," Lisa said as she brushed her fingers against a cream-colored satin A-cup, remembered days gone by and then looked at herself. "These don't belong on me. They have a promising career in porno. I have the measurements of a Louis the Fourteenth armoire. Remember the pencil test? Well, I can store a summer sausage under there, and a roll of crackers."

Her misery was enough to make me want to jot down a request for early, early menopause and submit it to my mother's prayer chain.

So by all means, it should have been her decision to name her next son what she wanted, but whenever we asked her, which was about three times a day, she still said she didn't know.

"What are we going to call my grandson?" my mother demanded from the dining room table. "Baby No Name?"

"I just don't know," my sister said again, flipping to the next page in the baby name book. "Nothing is hitting me."

"What about David?" my mother asked. "That's a nice name."

"Oh God, that's HORRIBLE," I said with a yell. "That's the name of one of my worst ex-boyfriends!"

"Is that the one you brought to my wedding with the electronic tracking device around his ankle?" Lisa asked.

"No, no, no. This was the one that said I was trying to trap him into 'nesting' because I left my eyeliner and a Janis Joplin CD at his house," I answered. "The guy with the tracking device was his roommate who was home when I went to pick them up."

"How about Paul?" Nana suggested. "Jesus had a friend named Paul and he seemed nice."

"No way," my other sister said. "Paul Crowder was the Booger Boy in my seventh-grade class. He saved his and looked at them under microscopes!"

"Yeah, that's a bad name," I agreed. "Paul DuBois in my eighth-grade class ate a retina from a cow eyeball we were dissecting because another boy bet him five bucks. They made him throw up in the sink, he got suspended, and in the end had to give the five bucks back, too."

"Here's one," my pregnant sister said, looking up from the book. "What do you think of Colin?"

"What kind of idiot name is that?" my mother spit out. "Why would you name a baby after a part of your butt? You might as well name him Rectum, because it's the same part of the body!"

"She said 'Colin,' Mom, not '*colon*,'" I tried to tell her.

"Thank God it's not a girl, you'd probably name her Sphincta," my mother shot back.

My sister looked puzzled.

"She means 'sphincter,' " I translated.

"That's what I said!" my mother responded in her native accent. "Sphincta!"

"I have an idea," I said, turning to my three-year-old nephew. "Nicholas, what do you think we should call your baby brother?"

After a careful think, he put his hand on his chin and said, "I think baby brother should be called P. V. Robin."

We all just looked at each other until someone asked him why.

"Um, Robin for Robin Hood from my new video," he explained. "And P.V. for P. V. Mall."

"I think you go shopping with Grandma too much," I whispered to him.

"Then how 'bout we name baby brother Disney Store?" he asked.

"I think you should name him Michael," my mother inserted. "An M name because he'll be born in the new MMMM-illennium!"

I just looked at her. "You didn't use your protein bingo card today on your new Weight Watchers diet, did you?" I asked. "Besides, your vote is null and void in this election due to the damage you caused when you named each of your daughters the most popular names for the year they were born and they *all began with the letter* L. You're disqualified for lack of initiative."

"I AM NOT a bad namer!" my mother protested.

"You are so, Mom," Lisa said from the couch. "Our childhood

dogs were named Bambi, Pookie, and Brandy. Those aren't dog names, Mom. Those are the names of girls who work at a place called Naughty Nudies."

"Besides, Mom, Michael was the name of the guy with the electronic anklet," I said. "As a matter of fact, he met his first three wives at Naughty Nudies."

Nothing really got solved that day, no epiphany was reached, no name was chosen, and my mother left my Nana's house saying, "M for Millennium! M for Michael! What *don't* you people get?"

Well, I still don't get it, but I do understand one thing. If the power of my mother's prayer chain isn't strong enough and I end up having porno boobs of my own, it will have been worth it when I hear my mother bring my kid to the mall for the first time and say, "And this is called the Disney Store, Sphincta."

Stolen

"Please sit down," my husband said as soon as I walked through the front door. "I have something . . . *disturbing* to tell you."

"Another cat died underneath the house," I said, taking a seat.

"No. The smell is still from the one that's already under there," he answered.

"You can't find the scissors again, so you trimmed your eyebrows with a lighter," I said as he just looked at me.

"Steak knife," he replied.

"Um, something disturbing . . . I know, I know! You accidentally put on a pair of my underwear and ended up liking it," I said, hoping that wasn't it, because although I can be cool with a lot of things, like unemployment, substance abuse, and chemical imbalances of the psychological kind, men in panties is not one of them.

He just furrowed his brow.

"Can you be quiet for a minute?" he finally said. "What I wanted to tell you is that someone—"

"—you know got all tingly when his wife's bra 'fell' on him," I said, shaking my head. "You tell him to keep Victor's Secret to himself because I don't want to know!"

"—stole your carport!" my husband released in one, rushed sentence.

I stood there for a moment, then sat back down.

"You are LYING," I said as I stared across the room. "That is completely unbelievable!"

It WAS unbelievable. The carport/shade structure was a good ten by ten feet, rose nearly nine feet into the air, consisted of metal tube construction and was covered by striped canvas, and was nearly big enough to park two cars under.

"I'm serious," he replied. "Somebody just hopped the fence and TOOK it. All of the gates in the backyard are still locked."

"Let me get this straight," I said slowly, thinking about it. What this meant was, essentially:

A) Someone scaled my six-foot block wall, THEN

B) pulled up the stakes that had secured the carport, which had been hammered a foot into the ground, THEN

C) tossed the shade structure over the wall as a whole unit (I know this because I put it together and knew that it would have taken nearly twenty minutes to disassemble in the dark making more noise than a drunk high school senior coming home past his curfew), THEN

D) ran down the street with what basically looked like a campsite with no fire, OR

E) threw the cabana into the bed of a waiting truck and stole away into the night to attend a BYOS (Bring Your Own Shade) midnight barbecue.

"Who steals a cabana?" I wondered aloud. "Picnic pirates?"

And if anyone saw this, did any of my neighbors think it was odd that someone was running down the street dragging a festive white-and-green-striped cabana behind him? Did they think it was the circus, or a disoriented parasailer?

And then I remembered where I live, and what lives several blocks from me. Oh yes, my neighbors. My fellow man. In fact, forty-seven of my fellow men were all living in the same apartment a couple of blocks away before the INS busted up that hoppin' party several months ago. On certain streets, it means you're rich if you have a broken, torn couch *and* a recliner on your front porch. By those standards, I suppose I'm the Bill Gates of my ghetto, flaunting my boundless and extreme wealth by pitching a carport in the dirt of my backyard. Shame on us, putting on airs. Filthy, greedy bourgeois!

How pretentious we were when we decided to remove asbestos and flaking lead paint before we moved into our house! Living like the kings of Fancy Pants Land, we were! That's right, we're too *good* for cancer and blood poisoning! But we snobs were sure taught a lesson when we arrived one morning and the house had been completely cleaned out, including the bounty of contaminated drop cloths and the bathroom sink. It was very unsettling to know that someone had been going through our things, and at that time, I wasn't sure whether it was more unsettling for me to have robbers or the DEA ransack my house (long story), because, in hindsight, I've learned that neither one comes back to clean up afterward. After the robbery, we used our air-conditioning savings to install a security system, and slept in pools of our own sweat for the next two summers.

My husband was admittedly being a show-off when he left a ten-speed with dented rims and two flat tires in our backyard, because someone also felt the need to relieve us of that little pot of gold. That's when we used our Christmas savings to get bars on the windows, and I was forced to give "Hug Coupons" to my family for holiday gifts.

Now comes the really sad part of the story. Pity the poor little thief who mistook the disintegrating circa 1985 Pier 1 wicker chair that was missing a seat for the ancient throne of Cleopatra, because despite its four unraveling legs, it had a little outside assistance walking off our porch. That's when I used the money I was saving for a trip to the gynecologist to get metal security doors and got a handheld mirror instead.

And, oh, what bravado we, Mr. and Mrs. Livin' Large, exuded by driving around in a truck with a dented, scratched tailgate, because someone also helped themselves to that morsel from the car part buffet, unhinging it from the bed and simply walking away with it. As a result, we started parking in the backyard, under the shade cabana I bought with my own money, money I had saved and earned from *working*.

That was an American Dream short-lived, wasn't it?

I'm not sure what to do now. Skip a mortgage payment and build a fire pit around my house, dig a moat, or smear something gooey and moist on top of the wall? Maybe I should take a tip from my old neighbor Frank, who laced his yard with trip wire that had "enough volts to knock a horse on its ass" after a seven-foot Barney Santa was shanghaied from his yard during Christmas of '95. Frank would also chop down trees in his front yard after he had fights with his wife, so I'm not too sure how realistic that option truly is.

An hour ago, though, I took a black Sharpie marker and wrote THIS WAS STOLEN FROM LAURIE NOTARO on everything I thought was worth more than ten dollars, including the replacement bathroom sink and a rug that smells like pee. Not that it would deter the kind of thief that was brazen enough to steal something as big as, say, *a bedroom* from my backyard, but at least I get the last word.

It's a disturbingly small reward, especially since someone out there still owes me a Pap smear.

Rolling Down the River

"HELP ME!" I screamed when I saw anything that looked like a hospital uniform pass me by.

I was nothing but a fool.

A big, dumb, yelping fool.

Had you asked me merely thirty minutes before if I thought I could hold it together if faced with a good deal of physical pain, I would have said, certainly yes.

Of course I could hold it together.

That's very important in those kinds of situations, I would add. It's almost necessary to have a certain amount of decorum and not scream and bawl like a ninny; that only makes things more painful. In fact, when I see people moaning, crying, and complaining on TV that they're hurt, it almost makes me want to laugh at them or possibly even hurt them myself for being such insolents. When you are in pain, you have to be strong; I should know. When I was in sixth grade, I was jumping rope when I fell and the cartilage in my knee tore completely, and instead of crying, I picked myself off the playground proudly and hobbled to the nurse.

Alone.

And in pain.

Without a sound.

Thirty minutes previous, that most assuredly would have been my answer. But now, as I gasped, reaching out to grapple at any pair of legs in teal green that walked within my reach and shrieking like a demon being doused with holy water, beaten with a crucifix, and pelted with Communion wafers, I clearly understood that pain had been a stranger to me. Until now.

Thirty minutes before, I had been standing in my kitchen when I felt something sharp stab me in my right side. It sucked the breath right out of me, and before I had time to recover, another stab hit in the same spot. In a moment, I was down for the count, screaming and writhing in pain.

Now, let me explain a little something about the sort of physical discomfort I was experiencing. It was a kind of pain that far surpassed anything I had ever felt before or documented on my 'Laurie's Random Pain Pangs' chart. This sensation made my "Cancer of the Upper Asshole" stab feel like the gentle, playful tickle of a peacock feather in comparison. In fact, it had my mind spinning, trying to decide whether it was possible that I was about to give birth to a pony via my belly button or had unkowingly been impaled by something, fearing that if I looked down I would see a pitchfork or perhaps a telephone pole protruding from my abdomen. Should you have been, at one time, ripped apart limb by limb by wild vicious dogs, a rather hungry lion, or the pack of women crowded in between the size seven-and-a-half racks at a Nordstrom shoe sale—while experiencing a charley horse cramp strong enough to cripple a nation—*and* you survived to tell the tale, you'd know a little something of the displeasure that was currently conducting itself in my body.

When my husband found me, I had somehow made it to the couch and was rolling from side to side as if I were on fire. Luckily, we live a block away from a hospital, so somehow, he got me to the car and within minutes we were in the hospital parking lot.

Now, even I, in my incredible state of agony, noticed the word EMERGENCY painted clear as day in huge block letters across the automatic sliding doors as we entered the hospital. However, I'm pretty sure I'm the only one who saw it, because despite the definition of the word "emergency," I've had shorter waits in the return line at Home Depot the morning after Father's Day. Truthfully, if we were to call a spade a spade and really be honest about what went on behind those doors, the word painted across them would not read EMERGENCY but REMEMBER: YOU'RE THE ONE IN AGONY, NOT US or HOPE YOU BROUGHT A GOOD BOOK, SOME SNACKS, AND YOUR OWN PILLOW.

It was going to be a bit of a wait.

There, sitting randomly in chairs across the crammed waiting room, was someone covering an eye as his remaining good eyeball stared blankly toward a wall, a girl in a cropped top holding her head between her knees as she rocked back and forth and moaned, and a wrinkled little man in a cowboy hat and a thin mustache holding a towel-wrapped bundle that looked suspiciously like a limb.

They had obviously been there for a while.

See, in my book, the word "emergency" kind of constitutes a sense of urgency, as in end-of-the-line urgency. It rarely ever gets more urgent than in the word "emergency." People go to Emergency because they assess their situation to be rather critical, they've determined that whatever is going on is not something they can handle or fix themselves, so it's about time to seek outside help. NOW. As in RIGHT NOW. Because honestly, the next level beyond "emergency" is a rather basic, no-frills drawer at the morgue with fabulous air-conditioning.

But to the employees of this emergency waiting room, it was obvious that the word "emergency" had kind of lost its gloss, its zip, its emergency-ness, as doctors, nurses, and people in latex gloves just strolled about as if they were shopping for paper towels at Target. No one paid any attention to the "patients" who sat and waited, and waited, and waited, cradling their possibly severed arms and trying to prevent their eyeballs from springing out of their heads like Slinkies. In fact, it's amazing to me that hospitals across the country haven't even tried to cash in on the basic needs of their waiting room patients by renting out camping equipment.

Because every seat in the waiting room was full, eventually someone plopped me into a wheelchair, but I hardly noticed. By this point, I was drifting in and out of consciousness in between my pitiful cries, like just after a night on the town in the good old days, except that then no one typically prodded me for my insurance card unless a spoilsport took signs of alcohol poisoning seriously and dialed 911.

Now, the next time I woke up, I was at the admitting station and my husband was fumbling through my purse for my wallet. When I came around again, the admitting lady was forcing a clipboard and a form with all of my vital information on it into my dead, lifeless hands.

"And please print clearly," she added sharply.

"Well, of course," I truly wanted to reply. "Naturally, making your job easier is my first priority at this time when the skeleton hand of death is inside my body, wringing my vital and tender organs out like a sponge."

Then she made me sign more papers than I did when I bought my house, to which I just started scribbling blindly all over. "And that one," she informed me as I scrawled over the last line, "gives your husband power of attorney."

"Dear God, do not plug me into anything," I managed to squeeze out as I shook my pen at her. "Don't even get me near an outlet! He's been waiting for an opportunity just like this since the day we got married."

I did the best I could under the circumstances, but honestly, that form looked like I had filled in the blanks with either my feet or a monkey proxy. Even I couldn't read my own writing, but as I tried to hand back the clipboard, a robust, full-throated moan was emitted from the waiting area, and I turned just in time to see the half-shirt girl—who had been clutching her head moments before—stand up, bellow again, and then crumple promptly to the floor. It was a maneuver straight out of a death scene in an eighth-grade play; the way her hand flew to her thrown-back head, the way her knees gave way first, the way she lay melodramatically on the floor, her hand still thoughtfully draped across her head as if she were a twelve-year-old Ophelia. Well, except for the part where a package of GPC menthol lights shot from her body, skidding across the floor, and her cropped top flew up, exposing one whole braless knocker that sported a rather large and confusing tattoo of either a unicorn or a donkey wearing a dunce cap.

Even though I felt unconsciousness creeping up on me again as agony was sinking its teeth deeper into my side, I knew this show was too good to miss. Suddenly, the emergency waiting room came to life, as if finally, FINALLY, they had a worthwhile emergency on their hands, a patient worth their training, as they gathered around the unicorn boob girl like ants around a bread crumb. Within moments, she was slid onto a flat board and a brace was looped around her neck, although I guess covering up her floppy, tatted booby didn't really fall into emergency care procedures, because the sagging donkey just kept winking at us as Ophelia was carried away on the stretcher. The stretcher had almost made it all the way to the ER doors when Ophelia opened her eyes, lifted her head, and cried, "Hey!! Isn't anyone going to get my smokes?"

She had faked it. You see, Good Old Uni-Boob had apparently decided to take matters into her own hands, and if the medical professionals weren't going to come to her, she was damn well going to make them. And she had given me more than a cheap look at her private parts. She had given me an idea.

"Help me!" I shrieked as soon as I saw a pair of booties or a paper hat come my way. "Please help me!"

After the first several professional medical people ignored me, I decided to start reaching for their legs, and screaming louder. I didn't feel guilty at all about demanding help; I felt I was simply vocalizing my pain. And I was. But I might as well have been sitting on a street corner, shaking an empty coffee cup and demanding change for my next fix for all the attention I got, which was not even so much as a stare.

Finally, I was admitted to the triage room, although I don't know how since I was pretty much unconscious. I believe I probably fell on someone passing by and they simply could not lift me off, so they just wheeled me in. When I came to, someone was struggling with my underwear, and I was almost alert enough to screech, "All hands on your own deck, buddy, it's not your birthday!" until I looked up and saw a lady.

This was the moment that my mother had devoted a majority of her lifetime to prepare me for; the time had finally come. And I had failed miserably. Earlier that morning, I had chosen foolishly. I had spotted a 1998 model, barely gray pair of panties in my underwear drawer, but instead had gone for the ones with little more than a rubber-band waist holding up something of a loincloth. As I had stepped into them and they flapped around my ankles like a hula skirt, I remembered thinking, "It's Sunday. Who is going to see these besides my husband? It's not like I'm going to be exposing myself to the world, is it?"

Now I had my answer. And it was YES.

This in addition to the fact that before I had left for the hospital, I was rather too busy fending off death to look for a razor and then use it on my, shall we say, most remote and secluded areas. In essence, the garden had not been tended, and was a bit in need of maintenance and something of a trim. I mean, really, I wasn't expecting that any strange company would be coming over, I've been married and off the market for some time now, so my OPEN HOUSE sign is rusty and somewhere in the garage behind the Halloween decorations and flat bicycle tires. Nevertheless, there I was, overgrown, unruly, and in combination with my castaway underwear, it was a wonder I wasn't ID'd as Sasquatch and sent to a kennel.

On my right arm, a nurse was digging around trying to find a vein like I was a fetal pig in AP biology class. In all honesty, with my cookie exposed to the world, my shaggy, gray shredded underwear sitting beside me like a mechanic's rag, rockets of pain going off in my abdomen, and a lady poking me in the arm with a needle so many times I could have qualified for methadone treatment on sight, I swore I had probably died at the check-in station and was now in my orientation session for my new lifetime/eternal membership in hell.

Pretty soon, I was sure, classmates from high school and old boyfriends would be passing by, commenting on my weight and how very poorly I had aged. How could this scenario be any worse?

The lady attempting to give me a homemade tattoo picked up my wrist and looked at my bracelet.

"Oh, look at that," she said. "You're that girl from the newspaper. Oh, oh, yep, here we go. Got a vein. There we go. I was beginning to think you were dead!"

"Could you please arrange that?" I replied.

And then, in a matter of seconds, all was peaceful. All was lovely, all was soft, and pretty and painless. All was as it should be.

I was on a Demerol drip. You could have brought cameras into that place, propped me up and shot away, and printed the gruesome image on top of every column that I wrote and at that moment, I would have let you. I would have *encouraged* it.

I was HIGH. I was really HIGH. I used to think I had pretty good connections, but none of my guys ever came through with anything like *that*. I was higher than I was in all of 1994 combined, and that was the year I was *totally* into Janis Joplin.

I smiled at my husband. "I want to take this stick home," I said, grabbing my rolling IV drip. "I want to keep it by my bed and just be happy and soft forever."

I could have sworn I saw tears gather in a rush in his eyes. "Oh, Doctor," he cried. "Thank you! Thank you! This is the girl I married! *There she is*! I haven't seen her this happy since she stopped self-medicating!"

"We think you have kidney stones," the doctor informed me, which was good news as opposed to hearing, "You're going to have a baby at any moment and you were just too fat and disorganized to know it!" or "You're incubating numerous alien reptilian embryos and they're about to burst through your rib cage in three seconds and then scurry into the hospital ventilation system. So hang on."

Kidney stones. How do you even get kidney stones? Could they be pieces of Bubble Yum that I've accidentally swallowed from my childhood, now fossilized and evil; Pop Rocks that never lived up to the "pop!" portion of their promise, and still retained their rock form; or little pieces of corn who thought to themselves, "Well, if I'm *never* going to be digested, why on earth would I want to go any further, where the lower you go, the worse it gets? There is a light at the end of the tunnel, but it's not a good one. Forget it. I just might as well stay here where it's warm, velvety, and purple. It's like being at the Artist Formerly Known as Prince's house"?

In addition, I didn't know what you do for kidney stones, or how you get rid of them, and all the people at the hospital did was give me a prescription for Vicodin and send me home. But my husband was smarter than that. Way smarter than that, and when we approached our freeway exit, he sped right past it and kept on going.

All the way to my mother's house.

When I woke up in her bed hours later, ice went through my veins. I was afraid that a version of my deepest, most horrifying fears had come true, which is that I have ultimately and tragically eaten enough sugar to force my body into a vegetative state and my mother takes me back in so we can finally have the close maternal relationship she has always craved, which consists solely of me not having the ability to speak and her picking out my clothes. Fresh from my Demerol daze, I knew it was only a matter of hours before my mom loaded me up in her van and took me to Wal-Mart so she could buy me several pairs of polyester short sets and back to the orthodontist to teach me a lesson for lying on my head-gear chart in eighth grade.

And then a little rolling stone inside my body began gathering no moss but was bouncing around like it was a pinball.

"MOM!" I yelled. "I need my drugs!"

"Keep your pants on, Courtney Love," my mother said as she doled out a Vicodin. "Which is more than what you did at the hospital from what I hear. You've had so many accidents with strangers seeing your coolie that I would wear shorts under *everything* if I were you."

I gulped it down.

"You hungry?" she said. "I made some nice tapioca pudding."

"Give me back that bottle, please," I said, reaching out my arm. "I don't want to live like this. I just can't do it."

"You just don't know how lucky you are," she replied. "There's a

Diamonique special on at two that lasts the *whole afternoon*! Maybe we can get matching earrings and a pendant set!"

For six days I was confined to my kidney stone prison, eating tapioca pudding, taking drugs, and staring into the toilet after almost every visit.

When six days had come and gone, my doctor finally decided I needed surgery immediately, but passed it off to his partner since he was going on vacation for a week.

Nervous about slicing open the kidney of a patient that he had never seen before, my doctor's partner called my mother and told her about his unease.

"This is what I propose," he said. "I'll prescribe Dilaudid for the pain, have Laurie drink as much water as humanly possible and lie with a heating pad around her side. If the stones don't pass over the weekend, we'll operate on Monday."

Three hours later, after drinking more water than the state of Arizona is allotted in a whole season and lying on the heating pad, I gathered with my mother and my father in the smallest room in the house. The three of us hadn't made a joint appearance in the bathroom since my whole family gathered around the bowl after my little sister swallowed a bicentennial quarter.

"Is that them?" my mother said, pointing.

"I guess," I said, shrugging.

"That's it? That's what they call a *stone*?" my mother asked. "That's what we've been waiting for? I expected a cashew, maybe a macadamia-nut-sized thing. A malted milk ball would have been nice. But that? A lentil could dwarf it!"

"I know," I said, rather disappointed. "I was expecting a comet. The stones in our Diamonique pendants are bigger than that."

"*Please*," my mother said to me with a disgusted look on her face. "If you bought these kidney stones on QVC, you'd get them twice as big for half the price. These are nothing!"

"I'm a little let down," my father said with a frown. "I expected more."

True, the pair of little stones nestled at the bottom of the bowl were nothing to boast about. But at least I got to go home and eat food of my own choice, and would be able to answer nature's call without having to scrutinize it.

And I still had a bottle of painkillers left to boot.

That, at least, rocked.

A Rolling Stone, Even When Sober, Is a Difficult Catch

Did you know that kidney stones are worth their weight in gold?

Well, of course you do. Apparently, every person in the world knows this but me, judging by the way my doctor was looking at me.

"You did WHAT with the kidney stones?" he asked for the second time in twenty seconds.

"I said I flushed them," I repeated.

My doctor just stared at me, then shook his head, as if he had just seen me pull my finger out of my nose.

"Can you tell me why?" he asked.

"Absolutely." I nodded. "If something leaves my body, I pretty much figure that my relationship with it has reached the end. Besides, I just got the last in the *Planet of the Apes* action figures on eBay, and there's no more room on the display shelf for any other collectibles."

Now, I wasn't sure if I needed to set the stage for him, but I should probably explain that the day my kidney stones made an appearance wasn't exactly a day of joy. After writhing in six days of the most incredible pain known to man, when those stones finally came rolling out, I named one Mick and I named one Keith and then I flushed them good-bye. There was no way I was about to reach into the potty and start pulling things out of it, I mean, there's no amount of pharmaceuticals that could ever make that seem like a good idea. Besides, I wasn't about to play with fate! The stones were gone, and the last thing that I wanted to do was keep them around for good measure, there's danger involved there any way you look at it. I mean, this is MY WORLD we're talking about, where it is quite feasible that Mick and Keith could have been mistaken for peppercorns and added to my food, or I could have popped them right into my mouth thinking that they were baby Coco Puffs.

My doctor, however, continued to stare at me.

"I've just got this thing about playing with my own tinkle," I tried to explain as a last resort, but he was having none of it.

"I'm not asking you to fingerpaint with it," he explained as he sighed. "But we need to examine a stone to find out what caused them and how we can prevent them. And according to these X rays, you still have one left!"

Damn that Charlie Watts! I thought, lagging behind and too mellow for his own good!

"This is a prescription for a diuretic," he said as he handed me the piece of paper. "Take these pills and drink lots of water for a week. And this time, catch the stone."

I nodded as the doctor started to leave the office.

"Wait!" I cried. "How am I supposed to . . . catch it? My reflexes aren't that sharp. I have problems catching a softball, let alone something the size of a Fruity Pebble."

"Go to a pet store and buy a fish net for an aquarium," he informed me as he left. "But you need to make sure to use it *every time.*"

Well, I guess I can do that, I thought to myself as I drove to the pet store. I guess I could pee into a little net. It wouldn't be so hard. Carrying it to the bathroom at work would be a problem, though, I suddenly realized, so I'll have to get a special little purse to hide it in.

At the pet store, however, I understood that a little purse wasn't quite going to cut it. In fact, it looked as if I was actually going to need a duffel bag, since the only nets in stock were easily large enough to capture a wide-mouth bass. Including the handle, some of the nets were the size of a rifle. Oh, that will be great, I said to myself. I'll just walk around the newsroom looking like Lee Harvey Oswald every time my bladder sends me a signal.

"Do you have anything smaller?" I asked the salesclerk. "I could have caught myself a medium-size second husband with this thing."

"Well, that's the standard net," he said. "How big is your tank?"

"Um." I thought for a moment. "Five gallons."

"And the type?" he asked.

"Freshwater," I added. "Or at least it usually is to begin with."

"Then that's your net," he said with a shrug.

"Okay." I sighed. "I'm just going to be honest with you. I need to pee in it."

There was a moment of uncomfortable silence between us.

"You know, ma'am," the salesclerk said as he shook his head. "I know the dog collars and the leashes may send out the wrong message to some people, but we're really not in the fetish business."

"Fetish? It's not a fetish!" I gasped. "It's medical!"

"Uh-huh," he scoffed. "Like I haven't heard that one before. It's not like you have gold up there or anything!"

"Wanna make a bet?" I snipped.

Back at home in my bathroom, the net was proving to be something of a challenge. Not only did I suffer scratches on the backs of my legs trying to find the appropriate catching position, but I didn't know exactly what to do with the net when my session had concluded. I knew I had to clean it somehow, but the thought of doing that at work was so horrible that when I fell asleep, I had dreams that kidney stones were floating around the office like butterflies, and I had to chase them with my net as I tried to run with my pants down around my ankles.

The next morning, I was attempting to shove the net into my purse when my husband saw it.

"Whoa," he commented. "By the size of that net, it looks like you won't be losing a kidney stone, you'll be gaining a bowling ball."

"Oh, that's it!" I cried. "I can't do this! I can't bring this net to work! What if someone sees me using this in the bathroom? I mean, I can only use the excuse 'Smile, you're on *Candid Camera*' so many times in there, you know?"

So I left the net at home. I figured if Charlie Watts felt like showing up at work, that was fine, but I needed to be able to walk around without people pointing and whispering in the elevators, "There's that nut job who plays with her own pee and thinks she's always on *Candid Camera*."

Plus, as it turned out, Charlie never made an appearance at all that week, and my doctor wasn't too happy to hear that when I had my next appointment.

"Well, that's quite unfortunate," he said with a deep breath. "We still need to find out why you're getting kidney stones. I'm going to need some samples from you."

"I'm game as long as it doesn't require a hook and bait," I replied, "or any other kind of sports equipment."

Down at the lab, the tech had just finished taking my blood when she asked me if my doctor had explained the "other" part of the sample.

"Just point me to the rest room!" I joked. "Believe me, I'm such a pro at that kind of sample that I don't even need a net underneath me anymore!! Ha ha ha!"

The lab tech gave me a funny look. "I don't think you understand," she said slowly as she pulled out something that looked exactly like a plastic gas can with a spout and everything. "It's a twenty-four-hour sample, which means everything for twenty-four hours goes into here."

I looked at the gas can, and I wanted to laugh, but I just couldn't. I mean, it even had a *handle* on it. Forget about the duffel bag, I was going to have to bring a *suitcase* to work. Now, not only was I going to be a pee handler, but I was a pee saver to boot.

I looked at the tech, who simply shrugged, and I could only think of one thing to say.

"Please tell me," I implored earnestly, "to look into that spout and smile."

Pain in the Assisi

The moment I saw it, I knew it was perfect.

The perfect Christmas gift for my impossible-to-buy-for mother.

Let's just say that it's a given that courtesy of QVC, whatever my mother wants, my mother gets, and typically within eight seconds of seeing it. My mother gets so many packages that she's on a first-name basis with the UPS guy and he knew the results of her last mammogram before my father did. However, there is an upside to my mother's passion for collecting abstruse gadgets. As a result, my sisters and I have begun a new family tradition on holidays called This Is Your Brain on QVC, in which we try to guess the purpose of any new QVC purchase, how many times my mother will use it, and how long it will be before she will throw it out. Last Christmas, it looked like she got nipple clamps by mistake, but after a lengthy ponder, she insisted that it was an accessory to bind the legs of the turkey while roasting that had a dual purpose as an eyeglass chain.

On the last scouting expedition of This Is Your Brain on QVC, my sister and I discovered these delicious-smelling muffins, which is what they looked like, but on closer inspection it was discovered that these were no muffins at all. They were candles. Muffin candles. I mean, they smelled like muffins, they looked like muffins, but eating them would have been like eating a Glade Solid or a stick of Mennen. So I was forced to ask her what they were, and she looked at me like I was stupid. "They're muffin candles," she said, much like she would say, "This is a candle. And this is a muffin." Separately, they're fine, I was dying to tell her, it's *together* that they're a problem.

So I said, "Well, why don't you burn them?"

And she said, "Because they're not for burning. Burning would melt them."

So I said, "Well, what are they for then?"

And she said, "To look like muffins."

So I said, "Then why don't you just get some muffins?"

And she said, "What, are you an idiot? You just can't leave muffins on the counter day in and day out without people thinking that you live like an animal! I don't want people running around town, saying that I keep the same old muffins on the counter!"

She was also very anxious to show us her newest arrival from QVC, which was some sort of food preserver/laminator thing. Everything she put in it came out looking like my employee badge at work, and you basically had to use a table saw or a blowtorch to get at the food once you "preserved" it.

"You can save ham for up to two years with this thing!" she said excitedly.

Now, I don't know if she has some inside scoop that the Three Little Pigs and Wilbur are now considered members of an exotic or endangered species, but to be frank, even if the last pig on earth were snorting his last breath at this very moment, I'd eat my own toes before I ate two-year-old ham that's really just a floppy pink fossil. I don't even want to drink water that's two years old, let alone something that died well before the last presidential election or when I had a whole different and much quicker metabolism. Plus the fact that she just completely ruined Easter for me; there's no way now that I'm going to trust any ham that she puts on that table. I'd have to carbon-date it before I even remotely considered taking a bite.

But this gift, the magnificent one I had found for my mother, was something she couldn't get on QVC, and as the clerk swiped my Visa, I couldn't help but smile.

"This is the last thing my mother would ever expect I would get for her," I said with a little laugh.

Only several days before, she had anxiously called me after her two-week trip to Italy, and frankly, I was surprised. Previous to her departure, she had informed me that the trip was not really a vacation but a pilgrimage to Assisi for the sole purpose of following in the footsteps of Saint Francis, and frankly, I couldn't resist making some fun out of it.

"A pilgrimage, huh?" I had asked. "You might want to buy Dramamine at Costco this time. You threw up for the whole three weeks of that Princess cruise, so sailing on the *Mayflower* should be a very enjoyable trip for you."

"That's not funny," she responded. "It's a religious mission and I'm going with people from church because your father got a little aggravated about my nausea on the last cruise and said the only trip he would ever take with me again would be out to dinner."

"Make sure to pack your buckle shoes." I giggled. "And a big white collar."

"This is nothing to joke about," she continued quite seriously. "We're staying at Father John's house and it's supposed to be clean, but I'll tell you right now, if I so much as spot a fly, I'm booking myself into the first Super Otto I find. The last thing I need is a big, filthy foreign Italian bug crawling into my head!"

"Hey, bring some beads to trade with," I added. "And don't forget your wampum!"

"I'm not laughing, Laurie," she informed me. "And Saint Francis isn't cracking a smile, either!"

So when my mother called when she came back, I was kind of shocked but very intrigued.

"Did you have fun on your pilgrimage?" I asked coyly. "Did you eat a lot of turkey?"

"I," my mother said slowly, "had a *wonderful* time. I had a *wonderful* time. For the most part. As long as I knew where I was, I had a wonderful time."

"What do you mean?" I prodded.

"Well, I got a little lost," she added quietly.

"You got lost in Italy?" I questioned, trying not to laugh.

"It's not that big a deal, it's just that when you suddenly find yourself on a dirt road in the middle of an Italian nowhere, dragging a heavy saint behind you and it starts to get dark, it's a little frightening, that's all," she replied.

"Do me a favor," I insisted, "and start from the beginning. I want the biggest laugh potential possible."

Apparently, during some time off from being a pilgrim, my mother and her friends decided to walk around Assisi, get a bite to eat, and then I'm sure secretly try to find a TV that had QVC on it. After lunch, they came upon a little shop in which my mother spied a statue of Saint Francis that she absolutely *had to have*. Because my mother hadn't purchased anything aside from a meal in approximately thirty-six hours, compulsion overtook her starved shopping-addict self. She suddenly found herself paying for Saint Francis, despite the fact that he was no ordinary little statue. No, no, no. How could he be? In his three-foot-tall glory, Saint Francis was a cast-stone, twenty-five-pound reminder of my mother's pilgrimage to the Holy Land and inability to access a twenty-four-hour shopping network.

When she and her friends left the shop with my mother's purchase in tow, they discovered that they had wandered into unfamiliar territory and had no idea of how to get back to Father John's place. One friend voted to try and retrace their steps, but my mother suggested getting on a bus since the town wasn't really that big and every other bus they had been on had stopped right in front of Father John's house. I'm sure that hauling around a religious relic as heavy as a couple of barbells had absolutely no influence on her desire to avoid hiking it back to their accommodations. Not at all.

So they got on a bus, happy to have someone take them to their destination. It was never really clear to me at what point my mother's blood pressure started to rise, but I would assume that it was somewhere around the time the bus had not only *not* stopped at Father John's house but had ventured out of town and my mother hadn't seen a house, a building, or a man-made structure for about fifteen minutes.

I think that's a pretty fair assumption of when she freaked out.

"I did *not* freak out!" she told me stubbornly. "I simply stood up and told the man he was going the wrong way. That is *not* freaking out!"

I was trying too hard not to laugh to answer.

"But he wasn't listening to me, either he couldn't hear me or he didn't speak English, so I figured it out in Italian," she told me.

Considering that the only thing my mother could actually decipher in Italian would be a menu at the Olive Garden and an assortment of unsavory phrases she learned when my relatives got drunk on holidays, I was eager to hear her translation.

"So I said to him, 'Papa Giovanni's casa THAT WAY,' and pointed back toward the town," she said. "Any idiot could have understood that. Right? Am I right? But he just kept on driving, so I said it a couple more times, and finally I went up to him and showed him. 'Papa Giovanni's casa THAT WAY!! Papa Giovanni's casa THAT WAY!' and I mean, it couldn't have been any more clearer than that. Honestly. I was pointing and everything."

Now, from what I understand, it was at precisely that point that the bus driver stopped the bus and, as my mother put it, "let us off."

"You got kicked off the bus?" I replied, unable to contain my laughter. "The bus driver kicked you off the bus?"

"I did not say that," my mother was careful to point out. "That is not what I said. I said he *let us off*. He stopped the bus, opened the door and . . . let us off."

"Oh, okay, sure, Mom," I replied sarcastically. "Where did this happen? Where did he 'let you off'?"

"Well, I don't think it was a regular stop," my mother said slowly. "There was no sign or anything. It was in the middle of some sort of field."

"A field? What kind of field?" I pushed. "A cornfield, or a field of poppies like in *The Wizard of Oz*?"

"How the hell do I know?" my mother snapped. "I'm from New York. A field is a field. I don't know what the hell kind of field it was! There were just a lot of leaves and things!"

"I suspect that this is where the dirt road comes in," I ventured.

"Yes!" she said excitedly. "He let us off on a dirt road. So we got off and started to walk, and after a little while—"

"You met a talking scarecrow and were attacked by flying monkeys?" I interjected.

"Anyway," my mother continued, "Saint Francis started to get heavy, and I couldn't drag him anymore, so we had to take turns. Finally, we came upon a café, but they were all watching a soccer game and nobody gave two shits that we were lost. So we went back out onto the dirt road and walked the rest of the way into the town, dragging that poor Saint Francis the whole way behind us, getting filthy from the dirt. I'm sure we looked like refugees."

"Well, naturally. If I was being run out of my home," I admitted, "the first thing I'd pack would be a midget-size concrete statue of a man in sandals and a hood cradling a deer."

"That's when I saw an American-looking man, and I thought, 'Thank God, finally, someone who will know where he is,' " she continued, ignoring me. "But when I talked to him, it turned out he was English!"

"You're kidding!" I exclaimed. "A European in . . . Europe?"

"You know what I mean," she hissed. "He pointed us right to Father John's house. And you'll never guess what."

"He was Prince Charles!" I guessed.

"Father John's place was just right around the corner from the shop where I bought Saint Francis, we just made one wrong turn," she said. "We were only a block away. Can you believe that?"

"I believe that vomiting isn't the only reason Dad won't go on vacation with you anymore," I said.

"But that's not the end of the story," she continued, and went on to explain that she put Saint Francis in her big suitcase, and indeed, he fit, since my mother travels like it's the turn of the century, with the modern equivalent of steamer trunks and a season's worth of clothes. She packed him carefully, with her softest clothes all around him to make sure he'd be safe for the trip home.

"But when I opened that suitcase when I got home," my mother related, "that Saint Francis had lost his damned head! Came right off and I found it rolling around in my underwear! Can you believe it? After I carried him on the bus and then dragged him all over that dirt road, he gets decapitated in my luggage! God help me. It's okay, though. Daddy fixed it with some superglue and you can't even tell."

So, after I signed the credit card slip to pay for my mother's Christmas present, you see, I couldn't help but laugh as the clerk looked round and finally came up with the biggest bag she had. After she deposited the gift into it, I nearly had to drag it to the car and then pulled a groin muscle so violently that I swear I heard it rip as I lifted the bag into the backseat.

It was all worth it, however, the moment my mom opened the big box I had wrapped for her. She fumbled around in the tissue paper and Styrofoam peanuts I had packed into it, and she smiled as she saw the foot of a sandaled man and realized the statue was holding a deer.

"It's Saint Francis!" she said. "Oh my God, it's a whole Saint Francis! Just like the other one, but whole!"

Then she leaned in closer to the box as she struggled to lift up the statue. "What's that?" she said, motioning to the tag that was tied around Saint Francis' neck.

She lifted it and read it: *If I have lost my head again, check in your panties, but don't worry. Daddy can fix me with some superglue and you won't even be able to tell.*

Not in My Lifetime

"Oh, thank God!" Nana cried as I opened her front door and walked into her living room. "I didn't think that anyone was going to come and help me! Oh, thank God, Laurie, thank God! I was so worried! I didn't know what to do!"

Honestly, my Nana didn't know the meaning of the word "worried." No, she did not. I, unfortunately, knew it perfectly well. Approximately thirteen minutes earlier, I had come home from shopping and played back my messages on the answering machine, only to find a harrowing recording of my Nana, who was apparently in some sort of agony.

It was evident that something was wrong immediately, since Nana's typical messages go something like this:

"Laurie? [insert silent pause that stretches out for four seconds, as if she's waiting for my answering machine to develop the intelligence necessary to reply: one thousand one, one thousand two, one thousand three, one thousand four] It's Nana. I don't want to bother you. [one thousand one, one thousand two] Am I bothering you? Laurie? It's NA-NA. Are you there? I don't know if you're there or not. Laurie? Maybe you're not there. Are you there? [one thousand one, one thousand two, one thousand three] I wonder when you will be home. Are you home? Huh. [one thousand one, one thousand two] Huh. Well, that's weird. *Click*."

The message I had just received was a different animal altogether, completely and entirely.

"Laurie!! It's Nana. NA-NA!! Are you there? Laurie? It's NANA!!! Oh no, oh no! Laurie, I need help! Help! [one thousand one, one thousand two, one thousand three, one thousand four] Oh God! *Click.*"

Naturally, I was a little unnerved. Actually, that's an understatement. I was completely freaked out and as I tried to dial Nana's number, my hands were shaking so badly that I missed several digits and had to redial, only to get a busy signal, which is what happens in the movies when the loved one you're trying to call back is just about to be attacked with a weed whacker by a serial killer.

Beep beep beep.

And of course Nana doesn't have call-waiting, because if she can't even remotely handle talking into a telephone accessory belonging to someone else, you can image the amount of damage she inflicted when she tried to operate one of her own.

For the three torturous, tense weeks that Nana had call-waiting, it was like Telephone Olympics in my family. The endurance required of all of us was simply inhuman, because she could absolutely not grasp the concept of a "beep in" or a "click over." She believes that beep to mean that her phone time has run out, her limit has been reached. Despite repeated efforts in Call-Waiting Counseling by my sisters and myself, if you were talking to Nana and she heard the beep, real or imagined, the next thing you'd hear is a click. She would simply vanish, believing if she heard a beep, and this was any beep, it didn't necessarily have to be coming from the phone (car alarms and the signal from the Emergency Broadcast System also fell into the General Beep category), she understood the conversation was over. This didn't mean, however, that she had successfully reached the other caller. If you were the one unknowingly beeping in on a preexisting phone call, you would immediately hear various numbers being pushed and a voice, roughly at least eighteen inches away from the phone mouthpiece, say, "—damn stupid thing, I don't know how the hell they talked me into this, how do you work it, is this the button you push? BEEP. Is this the button? BEEP BEEP. I'm pushing the button, is this working, hello? BEEP. THIS IS NA-NA!" and then hear the tones of a 7, maybe a 2, being pushed before she flatly hung up on you.

So we had to relinquish Nana's call-waiting rights. I mean, it had to be done. What choice did we have? Our nerves were shot. It was either kill Nana or kill the call-waiting, but something had to go. Then, my younger sister has the genius brain bubble to get Nana caller ID, and that didn't last long after we found out that Nana had been calling the phone company to complain that "Una Vailable" had been calling her incessantly and Nana had absolutely no idea just who that lady was. In fact, it was such a violation of Notaro Family Code that we nearly took away my sister's phone as punishment and a lesson to us all.

Beep beep beep.

With Nana's phone line busy for a consecutive seven minutes, I decided that there was no time to waste and I grabbed my car keys and headed out to the freeway.

I panicked the whole way there as several grisly scenarios shot through my head, but nothing could prepare me for the horror I found when Nana met me at the door. Not the thought of Nana being overcome by Clorox fumes as she vigorously scrubbed away on an already pristine bathtub; not the thought of one of her body parts or, if curiosity got the better of her, possibly an eyeball, getting sucked up by her Electrolux as she vacuumed her already unsullied carpet; not the thought of her getting nearly decapitated by the massive, plastic hinged lid of the community Dumpster after she tossed in her weekly contribution of "Who Needs This Crap?" which could very easily consist of valuable World War Two memorabilia, newspaper headlines documenting the last six decades' worth of historical events that my grandfather had spent years collecting, or even her wedding dress.

Nothing.

Because when I walked through that door, there stood my Nana, pale, clammy, and shaking, clutching the remote control in her hand.

"Oh God," Nana cried as she put her free hand to her head. "You have no idea what I have been through. No idea. I was just sitting here, watching the television about how New Orleans just had a big earthquake and now it's sinking when all of a sudden I heard a big noise outside! At first, I thought it was part of the story about New Orleans, because I tell you, was that a mess? That was a mess! People running, screaming, crying, bloody, all over the place! What a nightmare. Big crashes, like the one I heard outside, and Laurie, I tell you, no one was doing anything! The only one doing anything was James Garner, because he warned the mayor of New Orleans about this, way in advance, I guess he had a feeling about it, you know? But did anyone listen? No! And now, it was all up to James Garner to save the city and he was dragging a pregnant lady out of a burning building when I heard that big noise outside! He was at his friend Marty's party, too, when all of this happened but he left to save people's lives. But his friend Marty Graw's get-together was a disaster, just a disaster. Imagine having a party and all of a sudden everyone is bleeding and has broken legs? Poor Marty Graw! After I heard the noise outside, I went to the TV to see if James Garner had saved the pregnant lady, but my television was off and my electricity had gone out!"

Upon first hearing about the sad, tragic, and apparently avoidable destruction of New Orleans, my blood pressure shot up, but then I remembered who I was talking to.

"Okay, now when New Orleans had the earthquake on TV," I said slowly, "did you see Tom Brokaw, or did you just see James Garner?"

Nana paused for a moment. "What the hell would Tom Brokaw be doing in New Orleans?" she said, looking very puzzled. "Now how could he be there? I'm sure he had to be on the news that night, he can't be running around the country every time the ground shakes a little!"

"And you weren't watching CNN or anything?" I questioned.

"See An End?" Nana replied. "I don't know what you're talking about. I was watching television, I told you!"

"Lifetime Television," I added.

"It's Television for *Women*," Nana added proudly. "And I can't get it anymore! When the lights went out after the boom, the screen went dark. And now, the lights are back on, but my Lifetime is gone. It's gone and I don't know what to do! Help me get it back! Help me! The TV has been out for almost fifteen minutes and who knows what's going on in New Orleans by now! It may have sunk into the ocean, because James Garner said that was a possibility, you know!"

Honestly, I didn't really know what to do, but I knew I had a mammoth problem on my hands because after we revoked Nana's phone accessory rights, we all kind of felt bad, so we got her cable TV. It made sense that if all she had to work was a remote control, the disasters that resulted would be containable, hardly anyone, family members and strangers alike, could get offended, and it would occupy her at the same time.

And boy, oh boy, did it. Once Nana found Lifetime Television, hardly anything else existed. One-time staple favorites such as *Golden Girls* and *Touched by an Angel* (although the official Nana version of those shows are, respectively, *Old and Girls* and *An Angel Is Touching Me*) took a backseat to any movie starring the reigning HRH of melodrama, Susan Lucci, and also applied to court attendees Lindsay Wagner, Melissa Gilbert, Harry Hamlin, and Corbin Bernsen. If a baby-stealing ring was involved, even JAG (*Jack*) was in danger.

Now that her call-waiting no longer posed a threat to anyone, you could call Nana at any point in the day, ask her how she was, and she'd say, "Oh, me, I'm fine, but that poor Lynda Carter went to the doctor and guess what he did to her? A bad thing. *A very bad thing*. Oh God. No one believes her. But it's true, and now she's going to have a baby. *From the bad doctor*. I don't know what she's going to do. What a mess!"

"That's too bad," I'd reply. "Where did you see this?"

"On the television. *Crimes of Passion: She Woke Up Pregnant*," Nana says. "It's a *very* appropriate title."

Or you could be at lunch with Nana, and all of a sudden she'd feel compelled to tell you, "Oh God. Listen to what I found out. Remember that girl from *The Partridge Family*? The one who played the piano and then when she grew up she became a lawyer? You'll never believe what happened to her. She was a cocaine addict and then she was foolin' around with this fellow, and *bing*! she gets pregnant. Not married, not married. To make matters worse, the little bastard baby was born early and was a drug addict, too! Can you believe that? You would think she would know better, she was a lawyer, but no. I wonder what Shirley Jones said about that, I wonder."

"What a shame," I'd be forced to respond. "And you know this because . . . "

"Because of the television. *Love, Lies, and Lullabies*," Nana would say, shaking her head. "That says it all, doesn't it?"

Or I'd be talking to my mother or one of my sisters about a friend who, for example, was having trouble at work, and you could count on Nana to pipe in, "That reminds me of a lady up in Canada who was a truck driver who fought the mob because all of the men in her union were afraid to, but you know, how hard could that have been? Not to take away anything from her story, *Mother Trucker*, but you know, what kind of mobster lives in Canada? It's a very polite country and most of the people speak French. I could go and be a mobster there, that's how nice they are. I bet the 'mobsters' up there don't even kill anybody that gets in their way, they just crank-call them. Besides, how can you eat macaroni with a croissant? That's just disgusting."

Or you could arrive at Nana's house to pick her up for a family function and get roped into seeing the final, climactic moments of whichever movie she was watching.

"But you've seen *Baby Brokers* a hundred times," I once tried to argue.

"What, are you stupid?" Nana quickly shot back. "*Baby Brokers* is a show about Cybill Shepherd getting conned when she adopts a baby from a shady, unwed couple! *This* is *Baby Snatcher*, *that* is Nancy McKeon, and she pretended to be pregnant and then stole a baby! They are completely different stories! Cybill Shepherd would *never* steal a baby!"

"Maybe Lynda Carter could give Nancy McKeon her doctor's number," I suggested. "And then we could get to Mom's birthday dinner on time."

But it was no use arguing, and that, exactly, is how I ended up watching, almost in its entirety, a movie starring Tori Spelling and her croquet-ball boobs about a naïve girl whose two-faced boyfriend is a credit card thief, a liar, and, of course, a murderer. When her crafty, nosy mother discovers this and tries to break up the relationship instead of simply telling her daughter, her plan backfires and the boyfriend kidnaps Tori Spelling and takes her to a cabin in the woods in the cinematic magnum opus *Mother, May I Sleep with Danger?*

Forty-five minutes later, I was still sitting on the couch and had watched Tori spiral into a dangerous, blind sinkhole of denial, I was still watching as her boyfriend chopped down a log door with an ax to get to his beloved, and I was still watching as she then engineered her brilliant escape by hopping into a curiously and advantageously placed canoe and paddled down a river like Lewis and Clark, although Tori's river looked suspiciously like it was located in an amusement park in Anaheim.

It is worth noting that Tori Spelling completes the physical equivalent of a triathlon in this movie, although her boobs have about as much movement as a set of gravestones.

"God," even my Nana commented. "Her lentils look like they're bolted to her rib cage. No wonder she was paddling so fast. She's not afraid of tipping over. She'll never drown with those lifeboats under her chin!"

"I don't know how you can watch this stuff," I said blankly. "There must be something better on TV than this. You have almost a thousand stations!"

"This story wasn't too good, I agree," Nana relented. "Tori Spelling was much better in *Coed Call Girl*, even though she was a real slut then. She'd go with anybody, she wasn't picky. She should get together with that Partridge Family girl. Slut, meet slut!"

"I mean this station, Lifetime," I said, getting a little frustrated.

"It's like the Wounded Woman's Channel. Everyone gets chased, stalked, hit, becomes pregnant mysteriously, chased with an ax, or gets lured into a ring of prostitution. This isn't real. Just how many prostitutes have you known?"

"Um," Nana thought. "One."

"You have not," I replied. "You're talking about that one girl who dated your brother Frank before World War Two. She wasn't a hooker, she just wore red lipstick!"

"He met her in a bar," Nana said adamantly. "Pop Pop didn't meet *me* in a bar!"

"She was a *singer with the band*," I said. "That didn't make her a midnight cowgirl! What I'm trying to tell you is that this channel is crap. Can't you watch something else, like on the History Channel or Discovery?"

"Listen," Nana said sharply. "I'm eighty-six years old. I *am* the History Channel, and if there's anything on the Discovery Channel that I haven't already found out, I've been doing just fine without it. Believe me. Lifetime is television for women. They say it's empowering!"

"You're watching Tori Spelling paddling down a river with traffic pylons for knockers in *Mother, May I Sleep with Danger?*, Nana," I had no choice but to say. "If these women were empowered, they'd be making better movies!"

But really, there was no talking to Nana about upgrading her viewing choices to something palatable, or at least something that didn't have a "Chinese menu title," one choice from Group A (Deadly, Dangerous, or Betrayed) teamed with one choice from Group B (Lies, Kisses, or Love), for a name. I simply could not change her mind.

And now, as I stood in Nana's living room after getting her panicked message, I listened when she explained that her channel was gone.

"I tried to turn the TV on after the electricity came back, but all I get is this fuzzy stuff," she said as she pushed random buttons on her remote control as the screen went from one color of fuzzy to the next. "It's gone! It's gone! All of it is gone! Now I'll never know what happened to Marty Graw's party or if the mayor told James Garner he's sorry!"

"Oh," I said, understanding what happened. "Your cable has to be reprogrammed. I think all we need to do is turn your actual television to channel four and it should be fine."

Miraculously, the picture returned to Nana's TV, and she breathed an audible sigh of relief.

"Oh, thank God," she said. "I didn't know what I was going to do! I thought if my TV didn't come back on I might have to go to your mother's but that wouldn't work because she doesn't watch anything but QVC. And frankly, I can't stand that show. If I want to buy a blender, no one's going to force me to do it by putting a stopwatch next to it and yelling every five seconds that my time is running out! And the people that call in, oh my God, to talk about things they've bought. I think to myself, how boring does your life have to be before you want to have a conversation about a blender? 'You know,' I want to tell them, 'you know how stupid you look calling a stranger and talking about your pants on TV? "Oh, Kathy, I love my Bob Mackie stretch pants, they're so nice, they stretch when I sit down, and they dry so fast! I bought a pair in every color!"' What would make someone do that, I ask you?!"

"I don't know," I answered honestly. "Maybe her Lifetime TV went out, too."

"And your mother," my Nana went on, "You know, sometimes when I'm over there and she's watching that stupid show, I'll glance over at her and I can tell. She wants to call in. She has that certain look in her eye. She wants to call in and talk about her pants or her blender, too!"

Nana looked at me and shook her head.

"And last week, I asked her to lunch on Tuesday, and do you know what she said? She said, 'I can't go on Tuesday at noon. Kathy is having a show on Diamonique, the world's finest simulated gemstone.' I wanted to tell her, 'simulated' and 'gemstone' in the same sentence kind of cancel each other out. It's fake diamonds! Can you believe that? Can you believe that I raised a daughter who spends most of her time in front of the idiot box watching idiots and believing in fake stuff?"

"Who would have thought?" I simply answered. "Who would have thought?"

It's an Idiot Girl!!!

When I called my parents to tell them that after seven years of trying, I had sold my book to a publishing house, my mother reacted like I had just told her I had saved fifteen dollars off my grocery bill by using double coupons and a Fresh Value card.

"Well," she said. "That's very nice."

But really, I shouldn't have expected anything more or anything less. In my family, nobody wants to know anything unless you're fine, and if you're fine, then we don't need to talk about it any further. We're devout, practicing, sixth-generation Avoiders, so if you have any problems, you keep them to yourself because everything else is fine. So don't ruin it for the rest of us.

"After seven years, Mom!" I cried, trying to push it.

"*I know*," she replied. "That's what you said! I heard you!"

"*Seven years*, Mom!" I repeated, really trying to force the point.

"ARE YOU ON A CELL PHONE?" she yelled into her receiver. "ARE YOU IN A BAR? WHY CAN'T YOU HEAR ME? HAVE YOU BEEN SMOKING THE POT?"

It didn't matter, anyway. I knew my mom was happy. For the better part of a decade, she'd borne witness, as all of my family had, to my efforts to get my little book out into the world. Admittedly, I was a naïve columnist at my college newspaper when I had collected enough pieces to be considered a book. My book. A finished book. I thought that naturally, I had written a book, now I'll send it off to the publishing world and get this little book published. After all, why not? I'd gone through all the trouble of writing it! I sat down and printed out my sample chapters, letters of introduction, and contact information on very expensive paper, gently slid the packets into envelopes, addressed them to the seventy book publishing companies across the country, and mailed them off.

Soon, I was sure, I'd be hanging with Susan Sontag and Fran Leibowitz by the pool, chiding my new pals, "Another margarita for you, Miss Skunk? And you can go ahead and put your hand down, Frannie, you're not getting another gin and tonic until I see you in a skirt, you cuckoo!"

James Lipton's people would leave a message saying that although it's not standard protocol, they'd love to have me featured on *Inside the Actors Studio*. I'd start practicing my dramatic looks on cue whenever I heard tragic-sounding music and scribbling a short list of my most adored swear words, accompanied by a coy, shy giggle when I uttered them. In a shocking surprise that reveals just how much in-depth research goes into one of James's shows, he would demand a serious moment in which he would cock his head slightly to one side and say, "QVC? The first thing you bought with the money from your first bestseller was not a meat preserver, not Bobbi Brown makeup, not a trove of Diamonique, but QVC. All of QVC. And then you gave it to your mother. Tell us."

"Well, James," I'd say bashfully, "she just dreamed of having her own show on QVC, but the network said no. I mean, the woman just wanted to talk about her pants—and she's given me so much. She's a giver, you know. She gives and gives and gives. And I" interrupted by a swell of emotion—"excuse me, please. Just one moment, one . . . "—lengthy pause during which I look up and blink several times to regain composure—"and I just wanted to give something back to her. She's a religious pilgrim, you know. A *giver*."

And then, just when I had narrowed down my favorite profanities to twenty-four in preparation for James's show, I got to use every last one when I opened a thin envelope and read the letter from a renowned publishing house, one by one.

Each said I sucked.

Each said I was "not right for their needs."

Each wished me "good luck" in my pursuit to get my book published. And they meant it, the same way my mom meant it when I told her I had finally found a boy that liked me back.

"What does that mean, I 'don't fit their needs'?" I yelled into the air at no one. "The boy who likes me back once said the same thing, but a couple of drinks can change all that!"

Then, months later, I got a thick envelope in the mail. I clutched it to my chest, my heart churning, smiled, and raced inside my house to open it. I was ready to be redeemed, ready to tell James Lipton my whole painful story, which I had no doubt would bring him to his feet in a rage never before seen on Bravo. Inside, there was no rejection form letter, only a copy of my sample chapters on expensive paper that now had food stains and what looked like the remnants of a bloody nose covering the first page.

Then, because being a poor, chunky girl with bad skin and Arlo Guthrie hair wasn't a steep enough incline for a quick slip down my self-esteem slide, I repeated this ritual year after year after year.

And year after year after year, I still wasn't meeting anybody's needs except Hostess's and Marlboro's.

Finally, after seven years of trying to get my own book, I probably should have given up and adopted someone else's by changing my name legally to Anne Heche or Rosie O'Donnell, because they didn't seem to have any problem getting a book deal. All Anne Heche had to do was invent her own crazy-person language, run around a cornfield wearing only her bra, and try to talk people into getting on her spaceship. But then I had an idea. I decided to try my own brand of in vitro—I mean, after all, if no one else was willing to give me a chance, maybe I should just do a Wendy Wasserstein and go it alone.

So I published my own book, sold some copies, and then about nine months later, I got an e-mail from a girl named Jenny. She was a literary agent, had found my DIY book on her own, and was pretty sure she could sell it. I laughed and said I had been trying to do that very thing for seven years. If she wanted to give it a shot, I wasn't going to stop her, but I issued a supersized helping of "good luck" and didn't hold my breath.

Several days after Jenny sent out the book proposal, she called me and said that I had, indeed, finally fit someone's needs.

I was going to have a book.

So I called my family and told them the news, not even believing it myself. After my mother contributed her slightly less than stunning reaction, my dad got on the phone.

"Can you ask the fellow who said he'd print your book if he can put it in a spot near the *Auto Trader* at the bookstore?" he asked. "Because if it's next to the *Auto Trader*, that's the place to be. If I was a book, I'd demand to be next to the *Auto Trader*. Absolutely. That's when you know you've MADE IT."

"You know," I really wanted to tell my father, "retirement-aged men looking for a 1973 Ranchero GT with original paint, no rust, gold with orange/black stripes, 351C 2v, magnum 500's, AT, AC, PS, PB, new brakes and shocks probably aren't the typical readers for a book called *Idiot Girls*," but I refrained when I heard my mom screeching in the background that she just realized something and that she needed to talk to me again.

"Is your book going to be like Rosie's book?" she questioned. "My God, that woman is such a *giver*. Gives and gives and gives. Just like me. I'm a giver, you know. If it came up for a vote at our church, I'd make her a saint. I told all of my friends to buy that book *and look at how good it did*. Very good. I also want to know if your book will contain the F word, because you'd better not use F. "

"I'm pretty sure I didn't, Mom," I tried to reassure her.

"No F, you hear me?" she warned. "Because if you do, I will not tell any of my friends to buy your dirty porno book. And *then* where will you be? You'll be F'ed! How do you like that? Rosie didn't need F in her book! That woman is a giver, you know!"

"I know, Mom," I agreed. "Just like you."

Prude vs. Nude: Why I Hate Kate Winslet

I don't believe it, but I think I just might actually hate something more on the face of the earth than Kate Winslet.

See, my husband has a big thing for Kate Winslet, so big that I have been forced to watch *Titanic* an unnatural number of times, despite the fact that I have repeatedly suggested that we just fast-forward to the part where she gets naked. Oh, sorry, honey. I meant, "nude."

Anyway. I've seen every Kate Winslet movie ever made, and let me tell you, that was no picnic. Harvey Keitel is in some of them, you know, and he starts losing clothes, too. I had to eventually revoke my husband's Blockbuster privileges. I mean, you imagine yourself sitting on the couch in your elastic waistband pants while she's taking off her top AGAIN. I can't compete with that. There's only so much tummy sucking you can do before gravity wants its rightful place back. I thought we had found a happy compromise when *Iris* came out; after all, it's about an old writer dealing with Alzheimer's. There's no room for nudity with that plot, I thought, but believe it or not, the title wasn't even on the screen yet before a pair of nipples made an appearance swimming underwater, and guess who they belonged to? I'll give you a hint: the smile on my husband's face could not have been bigger if he had just inhaled an entire tank of nitrous oxide.

In any case, I will put my loathing of Kate Winslet aside to embrace my new object of contempt: the Rapiscan Secure 1000. That's right. The "virtual strip search machine." Tested at Florida's Orlando International Airport, the Rapiscan Secure 1000 is a low-level X-ray machine that zaps just enough radiation at you to scan through your clothes—and stop at your skin. Just enough so that you pop up on the screen NAKED. And I'm sorry, because it's not nude if you're not Kate Winslet. It's NAKED.

I just want to ask, how is this a solution to the security problem? Because all it sounds like is some freaky guy fantasy to me. It's like this ex-boyfriend of mine who I don't believe I ever saw sober in the four months we "dated" (translation: I drove him places, like to the bar, to the liquor store, to court), whose answer to every problem was, "Dude, let's get naked." It was gross and it was bad and I broke up with him after I drove him to the mall and he got it printed on a T-shirt.

I'll tell you one thing, and I wanna scream this loud enough so that the airlines will hear this and put up a stink about it: If I have to go through the security checkpoint NAKED, I JUST AIN'T GOING THROUGH. I am not. Anyplace I can't drive to on vacation I will visit through the magic of cable TV, because if there's one thing I fear, it's not talking in front of a large audience, it's not meeting my maker when it's time, it is being naked in an airport. I will never fly again if it requires my image—life-size, mind you—popping up on a screen with no panties, no bra, and not even protection from my hands to separate my battle with gravity from the outside world. I'd rather ride to New York in a *stagecoach* than subject myself to that. In fact, I only know of one person who would meander happily into a naked scanner.

And all of you airlines, I really hope you're listening, because I'll tell you one more thing: One lone Kate Winslet cannot support an entire industry.

Putting the "Die" in "Diet"

I knew exactly what I was doing. I had given the matter a great deal of thought, and my words were deliberate. I knew I was about to cheat.

"I really need you right away," I quietly stressed to the man on the other end of the phone, while my husband sat in the living room, watching TV. "It's an emergency! I have to see you soon. Please HURRY!!"

"Okay, okay," the man agreed, and hung up.

I walked into the living room and flashed my husband a quick smile.

"What do you want for dinner?" I asked, without any trace of my deceit.

He looked at me disgustedly. "No more meat," he said simply. "I can't eat any more meat."

I knew how he felt. I was really sick of meat, too. Ever since we had started a high-protein, no-carbohydrate diet two weeks before, we had eaten more meat than the entire Clan of the Cave Bear in one hunting season. We learned about the diet from our friends Jon and Kevin, who had lost an amazing amount of weight in just two weeks by cutting out bread and sugar from their meals. It sounded like a dream. Eat all the cheese, butter, cream, and meat you want, and watch the pounds drop from your butt like fleas off a hairless dog.

After thinking about it for fifteen minutes and deciding that we were prime candidates for this diet, I sprung it on my husband that we were going to start the following Monday to lose the twenty pounds we had gained during the course of our marital bliss. I stocked the fridge with roasts, chops, steaks, and cheeses, some from animals I'd only seen on the Discovery Channel.

During our first dinner, we were enthusiastic. Hovering over our plates piled with steak, we dug in, convinced that each mouthful of flesh got us that much closer to wearing old jeans. In that first week, one, two, three, four pounds magically disappeared while we slept. I had visions of myself in three weeks' time, wearing a cute little sleeveless J. Crew dress without the disturbing presence of the two swags of flesh that live under each of my arms and are big enough to pull across a movie screen. I had dreams of tucking my shirt in, and actually fastening a seat belt in the car without bumping into my belly baguette first.

We chewed and chewed and chewed. Five, six, seven, eight pounds floated away. Life without bread and sugar was indeed nearly empty, but watching the scale drove me on.

"Honey," I asked my husband a week and a half into the diet, "pick me up to see if I feel lighter."

"No," he said tiredly, almost in a whine. "My shoulder still hurts from picking you up yesterday."

"Come on, pick me up," I coaxed. "Pick me up like those dancing kids on the Gap commercial. I'll kick my legs this time!"

During the second week, however, things were beginning to drag, even though we had both lost twelve pounds. We had eaten enough meat that we should have been branded and pierced with an ear tag. Our back molars had been ground down to the size of Tic Tacs. I knew things were bad when I passed a Taco Bell and my mouth watered, but my desperation was sealed after I saw a fat family buying a bag of pretzels at Safeway and I burst into tears. I was ready to quit the diet and lose the remaining eight pounds by shaving my legs. Frantic, I called Jon and Kevin for support.

"Don't give in," Jon urged me. "Be strong. A lady at work lost so much weight that she looks like Karen Carpenter. Now put down the box of Oreo cereal and get yourself a nice ball of mozzarella."

"If you need a treat, make the recipe we gave you for Cheezy Beef Popsicles," Kevin suggested. "That will pep you up!"

"How can anything pep me up?" I questioned. "Because of all the cheese and meat I've eaten, I haven't gone number two since August. I'm a walking septic tank!"

"Maybe she's eaten too much meat," I heard Jon whisper to Kevin. "This sounds like mad cow disease."

"I don't need to be shot," I hissed into the phone. "I just want to eat a roll. I found some hot dog buns from the Fourth of July on top of the refrigerator. I'm going to take a bite!"

"Step away from the buns!" they both shouted over the phone. "We're going to talk you down. Put your hand to your face. Push in. What do you feel?"

"The nubs that used to be my teeth," I answered.

"Go higher," they said. "Now what do you feel?"

I did feel something. "I don't know what that is," I replied. "It feels . . . hard. And it's kind of . . . round."

"IT'S A BONE!" they said. "IT'S A BONE!"

"A bone?" I said weakly. "I have bones in my face?"

"Yes!" Jon exclaimed. "And you have more! They're all over your body!"

I looked at my hands. I saw BONES. At my elbow. BONES. Right under my neck. BONES.

I had BONES.

And this was what I was thinking as I hung up with Jon and Kevin and dialed another number with my bony fingers, telling the man at the other end that it was an emergency, and that I needed to see him right away.

He didn't disappoint.

Within thirty minutes, he was at the door, knocking. I took the box from his hands. "I knew I could depend on you," I told him earnestly.

"It's only a pizza, lady," he said.

My husband looked stunned. "A pizza? You ordered a pizza?" he stuttered.

"Yes," I answered without flinching. "We have suffered. We deserve this."

"I've seen a lot of weird things, lady," the pizza guy said. "But I've never had anybody order a pizza without the crust."

My husband just looked at me, his hand on his head.

"Keep your hand right there," I said to him. "Now push in."

"The Sims"

"What is that?" my husband exclaimed from where he stood behind me. "What IS THAT? What is that thing right near the fireman's foot in the front yard? Oh my God. *Oh my God.* What . . . what *have you done?!!*"

Honestly, it really wasn't my fault. Things in my environment had gotten a little bit out of my control, as things sometimes do. I mean, we can't control every little facet of our world all of the time, and I was trying to tell my husband that when he pointed toward the fireman's foot and yelled again.

"Look at that! It *is* your fault!" he insisted. "That fireman is giving me the most disgusted look I've ever seen."

I don't know, maybe it really was my fault. After all, after my husband bought me the computer game called "The Sims," the clerk at the Apple store was very careful to give me a stern warning as he handed my new game over.

"Now, since you get to create your own characters in this computer game, many people are tempted to duplicate themselves and their spouses," he said cautiously as he looked me in the eye. "DON'T DO IT. No matter how tempted you are, DON'T DO IT. You'll almost always end up getting divorced."

For those of you unfamiliar with this game, briefly, this is the point: You create people, build houses for them, create a neighborhood, and watch how they coexist domestically and within the neighborhood. In short, it's like making your own soap opera, and you get to play the almighty deity and Grand Puppetmaster, which I wish I could have chosen as my major in college. Wow, I thought, this is a powerful game, as I walked out of the store, went immediately home, popped in the game, and promptly created a Laurie character and a Laurie's Husband character.

Now, it's not like I wanted to prove the store clerk wrong by insisting that our marital bond was deep enough to forge through a computer game without involving simulated lawyers, but I do have to admit that he planted a seed. I mean, it certainly was tempting to see what would happen between Laurie and Laurie's Husband when left to their own devices—if they got divorced, if they stayed married—it was like watching an ant farm, in a sense, only the ants had human heads that looked like you and your husband. Plus, being the empty, self-centered person that I am, how could I possibly resist spying on myself in 2-D? I mean, honestly, what was the worst that could happen?

I went to work at making myself and my husband. I picked physical characteristics that resembled our own, except that I thought my character should be most representative of Laurie in Her Prime, which included skinny upper arms, a single chin, and a belly that didn't need twenty-four-hour suck-in control, because frankly, I'm rather busy at all hours of the day trying to rope in my own abdomen, let alone the big, fat, floppy breadbasket of an imaginary me.

Then I made Laurie's Husband, and I was pretty nice to him, too, except that I didn't want to make him too nice and appealing, fearing that might raise his fake self-esteem level to the point where he might have the inkling that he could get a better fake wife than Laurie in Her Prime. So I gave him a little bit of a belly. Just a little. Just a tiny, little, teeny belly. So teeny it was almost not even visible underneath the shirt with armpit stains, but kind of visible through the tears in it. Then, for a moment, I thought about making him bald, but ultimately I gave him a mullet, so savage and yet so free, instead for maximum marriage insurance.

When creating our personalities, I really did try to stay as faithful to the truth as possible, giving us the appropriate amounts in the required areas of neatness, niceness, playfulness, activity level, and outgoingness.

Now, truth be told, neither I nor my husband is very neat. We are not tidy people. At any given time, there are dishes in the sink, abandoned shoes in the living room, junk mail on the dining room table, the ironing board will not be put away, and there is the constant presence of a single roll of toilet paper that appears to simply roam about the house on its own. If you come to our house unannounced, we will probably not let you in, although it's more likely that we will pretty much ignore you altogether. Last week, someone knocked on the door, and I foolishly stepped into the living room just in time to see a person, tall and eerily resembling my husband, peeking in the windows. I froze, backed up slowly, and scampered to the bedroom, where I hid from my mother-in-law for a full eight minutes before she had the good sense to simply get back in her PT Cruiser and go away. *No way* was I letting her in. *No way.* There were three loads of unfolded laundry heaped on the couch, a very dead poinsettia she had given us rotting away on a sidetable, a blanket of dust almost thick enough to smother Pompeii over everything, plus a sinister, mysterious poopy smell whose source had eluded me for several days, despite an entirely vigorous hunt in which I was armed with a stick, a flashlight, and a pair of barbecue tongs.

As far as niceness goes, well, I guess you could say that Laurie's Husband got far more nice points than Laurie did—after all, what kind of person hides in a bedroom gnawing away on a Milky Way bar while her mother-in-law is rap-tap-tapping on the front door for four hundred and eighty endless and tortuous seconds? Not a very nice one, I can tell you that.

When it came to "playfulness," I have to admit, I didn't even know what the hell that meant. Playfulness? If that meant only being able to stumble through your days at your place of employment by pretending it was a madcap sitcom complete with a laugh track in your head, I guess I was playful. The same with the "outgoing" characteristic. In my opinion, the creators of this game wasted a lot of space by giving the players doltish characteristics, listing "playful" and "outgoing" when I didn't see one single option for "resourcefulness" (being of sound enough mind to stave off credit collectors by paying a credit card payment with another credit card) or "trickery" (being a quick enough thinker to pretend that you've died when credit card people call to belittle you and try to force you to pay them when all cards are currently in a state of "denial").

Personally, if we were being really truthful, I really think the game should have also had a category for deafness, since that's the claw that slashes at a marriage first. My husband went selectively deaf approximately twelve hours after we took our vows (i.e., around the time he woke up and realized what he had done). I know now that if I say something and get a "What?" from my beloved, I'm already miles ahead of the game since 90 percent of the time I simply get a blank stare. It took me almost seven anniversaries and a chapter in a child psychology book to make myself heard, which I've learned entails shouting out a word that he recognizes first, like "BEER!," "BOOBIES!," "VIDEO GAMES!," or "KATE WINSLET!," and once I've got his attention, I can toss him the dead poinsettia with the words "Your side brought it in; you take it out."

But there is no category for deafness or trickery in "The Sims"; they apparently subsist on playfulness, niceness, and count on a lot of outgoing activities to move the game along, which I decided was going to be very boring. It was going to be like living in a Mormon settlement, but without polygamy to spice things up.

After I created Laurie and Laurie's Husband, I moved them into a house and started the game. Now, on a control panel toward the bottom of the screen, all of the characters' needs are documented, along with how well those needs are being met. There are eight basic categories: "hunger," "comfort," "hygiene," "bladder," "energy," "fun," "social," and "room," which indicates how tidy and livable your house is. So as Laurie and Laurie's Husband walked around in their house, it was my job to take them to the bathroom when they needed to pee, make sure they ate when they were hungry, make them take a shower when they got dirty, go to sleep when they got tired, and clean up after themselves. In short, it was like having an electronic pet, and to tell you the truth, I was not truly finding the game a whole lot of fun at all. It was like taking care of kids! Feed me, watch me, wipe me. Where was the action, where was the pull, the attraction to this game? I didn't know, but I was hoping that if I took Laurie and Laurie's Husband to the potty enough times, they would kind of get the idea and then more interesting things would begin to take place aside from having a game that consisted solely of all of the most boring elements of my own life.

One thing is for sure, however; Laurie and Laurie's Husband were *pigs*. And I mean *pigs*! When she was done eating, she would simply throw the food on the floor, and one time I actually caught him leaving a turkey leg in the front yard. *In the front yard*. Okay, it's true, I gave him a mullet and armpit stains, but the last thing I expected was an automatic lapse into "Livin' in the Holler." They left such a mess that flies were buzzing all around the house, and what I believed to be stink lines were waving before my eyes on the computer screen. Finally, I made them get jobs—which, in the Sims' world, is as easy as picking up the newspaper—but making sure that both of them were up, washed, dressed, and fed before the car pool came was nearly impossible. After I would wake up Laurie's Husband, I'd be getting her ready and off to work, only to find out that he went back to sleep, *just like in real life*. Eventually, after missing his ride to the office for *three days in a row because it was impossible to get him out of bed*, he lost his job, and really, who could have been surprised at that? Who? I could have told you that was going to happen. Anyone could have seen that coming!

Laurie, it was obvious, wasn't too happy with him, either. She came home from work, found the house buzzing with flies, him watching TV, a pile of turkey legs by the front door, and she started stomping her foot and shaking her fist at him. He retreated into the bedroom, where he sat on the edge of the bed, put his head in his hands, and began to sob.

Oh, this is ridiculous, I thought, so I decided that he definitely needed to get another job, one he was actually going to go to this time. So I made him get the newspaper, and then, to my surprise, he looked at me, a bubble came out of his mouth, and there were words inside it that said, "I don't want to look for a job right now. I am too depressed."

And then he gave me a sad face.

I, frankly, did not know what to say. I was shocked speechless.

Too depressed? You're too depressed to get a job, huh? I thought. "Well, that may have worked in real life, buddy boy, but this is MY game and I AM THE GRAND PUPPETMASTER," I yelled at the computer screen as I made Laurie's Husband pick up the paper again. "I will do in my pretend universe what I apparently cannot do in reality! I command you to get a job!"

And again, as if I didn't understand him the first time, he informed me that he was too depressed to get a job. Then he shook his fist at *me*. And I mean *the REAL me*.

"Who are you commanding to get a job now?" my flesh-and-blood husband said as he came into the room and looked at the computer screen. "Who is that fatty? Look at him go! He really wants to punch you out! Without the gut, he looks like Shaggy from *Scooby-Doo*."

"No," I said, trying to make Laurie's Husband pick up the newspaper again. "It's not Shaggy. It's you."

"Oh, great," he said. "You made me a barrel-shaped, Schlitz-guzzling mechanic so I wouldn't cheat on you, huh? What is up with my hair? I look like a member of REO Speedwagon."

"I'm just trying to control my simulated universe," I tried to explain as Laurie's Husband took the newspaper and threw it on the kitchen counter, narrowly missing a growing colony of flies that was starting to resemble a small tornado.

"And who's that?" my husband said, pointing to the screen. "That looks like Julia Roberts."

"Why, thank you, kind sir," I said, beaming. "That fetching vixen is your lovely bride."

"I get to be married to Julia Roberts in this game?" he asked. "She's okay, but she's really not my type. Do they have a Kate Winslet type? Can I have Kate Winslet? I want a Kate Winslet."

I just looked at him. "That's not Julia Roberts, it's me!" I heartily informed him. "And no, they don't have a Kate Winslet, mainly because people keep their shirts on in this game. Kate Winslet would feel very out of place, I'm afraid, being on-screen and not popping out her boobs at least once."

"In *Iris* she was *underwater*, Laurie, so that *hardly even counts!*" he replied.

"If I see an areola and a nipple, it counts, all right, whether it's blurry or not," I argued back.

"Why is the REO Speedwagon Shaggy threatening you with physical violence?" my husband asked. "And why is he crying?"

"He's depressed," I offered. "He lost his job and now he's too depressed to get another one."

My husband is far more familiar with computer games than I am, mainly because when the deadline for my first book was rapidly approaching, I knew he was too old for day care and we didn't have enough money to send him somewhere for the whole summer, so I did the next best thing. I went to Costco, found the "Battle Chest" version of the "Diablo" computer game, gave it to my husband, and I didn't see him again for three months. It didn't take me long to understand that computer games just may be the cure for domestic hostility, and that the nuclear family could stay nuclear as long as there is a PC in the house with a CD drive. Daddy and Mommy don't need to get a divorce; Daddy just needs to get "Diablo." This way, Mommy will never see him again as long as she lives, but his paycheck will still pop up in her checking account twice a month. You see, as long as there's fire, weapons, and the occasional hope of spotting a scantily clad figure with hips (even if she is trying to impale him with a javelin like a rotisserie chicken) a man will stay chained to that dream as long as you let him. And, as a result, I met my deadline.

"Oh," the expert said, pointing to the Sims' needs barometer at the bottom of the screen. "He's not doing well. He needs to socialize, to clean up, and he's hungry. Maybe if you make him do those things, he'll be happy enough to get a job."

"It would be easier to slip him Prozac, but I'll try it," I said. "Maybe they can socialize and have fun while they make dinner together."

"Good idea," my husband agreed as he pulled up a chair next to mine and sat down.

So I put Laurie and Mr. Sad Sack to work in the kitchen to interact and raise his spirits, and everything seemed to be going fine. I made her tickle him, which he liked, and then she told him some jokes. His "fun" level was rising, which was a very good sign. Laurie was making dinner, things were looking up, and at least he had stopped crying. I thought things were going well, until my husband pointed to the computer screen and said, "What's . . . that?"

At first I didn't know. It took me at least a couple of seconds to realize it was a fire. It was a fire because Asshole Sad Sack had put the newspaper too close to the stove where Laurie was making dinner, and a small fire had erupted. And Laurie and Laurie's Husband were just standing there, watching it.

"I don't know what to do!" I said in a panic. "I don't know what to do! What should I do?"

"Um, do you have a phone?" My husband said from behind me as he moved closer to the screen.

"I don't know!" I cried.

"There it is!" my husband pointed to a phone on the kitchen wall. "Make them pick up the phone to call 911!"

I clicked on the phone, and clicked, and clicked, and clicked, but neither one of them made a move. This was primarily because Piece of Shit Sad Sack just shook his stupid head and gave me another sad face, and Laurie couldn't get to the phone, well, because Laurie was now entirely engulfed in flames.

I started screaming.

"I'm on FIRE! I'm on FIRE!!" I yelled as Laurie batted at the flames that were surrounding her, and then as she really started to freak out and called out to *me* for help.

I was still clicking on the phone, and I searched the screen frantically for a garden hose or anything to put the fire out.

While Laurie's Husband, the one who actually *lived* in that house and was to its same scale, so he could see things far more clearly than I—I mean, really, I'm a giant in this world, the whole house is about a foot across, and being a giant sometimes does *not* give you a vantage point, contrary to popular opinion—just stood there, Laurie's arms were flailing about, and she was yelling and hollering. The flames were almost out of control now, the entire kitchen was ablaze (except for the area that Bastard Son of a Bitch Sad Sack was observing from a corner). Frankly, I was about to throw my Diet Vanilla Coke right on the screen when my real husband suddenly had an idea.

"Click on the flames!" he yelled. "Click on the flames and see if you get an option!"

Immediately, I clicked on the flames, and what popped up but the option to extinguish, and that's when Sad Sack finally coughed up a goddamned fire extinguisher and sprayed it all over the kitchen. The fire subsided.

But it was too late.

A computerized version of the Death March was heard, and when the fire extinguisher spray had cleared, Laurie was gone. Where she had stood just moments ago, batting at the flames licking at her tiny simulated body, was now a small, gray urn.

"Oh my God," I said quietly.

A message from the game popped up on the screen.

"Laurie Notaro has died," the box said.

"I'm . . . dead," I said weakly. "I'm dead. I died. I DIED. I am DEAD!"

"No way," my husband whispered.

"How can I be dead?" I questioned.

"Oh, man, demons eat me all the time in 'Diablo,'" he said. "One time, I was mauled by evil devil strippers. It was gruesome, but also strangely erotic."

"This is all his fault," I said, pointing to Laurie's Husband. "You! This is your fault, you lazy, stupid asshole! You just stood there as she sizzled like a Jimmy Dean sausage link!"

"Click on the urn," my husband offered. "Maybe there's a way to bring you back."

So I clicked on the urn, but the only thing that happened was that an option to "mourn" popped up. So I took it.

And then, a beautiful thing happened.

Someone started to cry. But it wasn't simply crying; it was more like heart-wrenching, pain-filled weeping, almost as if your soul had been ripped from you, or worse, in this case, your meal ticket. Like if the only person in your house with a job was suddenly transformed into a pile of talcum powder that could fit into a can of fruit cocktail.

"I'm . . . *crying*," my husband said simply, pointing to Laurie's Husband as he wandered about the filthy, charred, trash-strewn house. "I'm so sad."

"Look at that," I said unbelievably. "Look at that bastard cry."

"HOO HOO HOOOO!!!! HOO HOO HOOOOO!!!" Laurie's Husband wailed.

I clicked on my urn again. Mourn. And again. Mourn. And again. Mourn. Again. Mourn. Mourn. Mourn. Mourn. Mourn. Mourn.

"Cry, you big baby, cry!" I commanded. "Look what you did to her! Look what you did! I'm going to keep you so goddamned depressed you'll never be able to get a job, have a normal life, or marry anyone else! Do you hear me? Cry! Let me hear you cry!"

He deserved it. You know he did.

That's when the fireman finally showed up, and Laurie's Husband moaned all the way out to the front yard to greet him as the fireman stood next to a bunch of decomposing turkey legs.

"HOO HOO HOOOO!" I made him say to the fireman. "HOO HOO HOOOO!!"

"Come on, quit clicking on the urn," my husband said. "I've been through enough. Don't you want me to get on with my life? Hey, can we make a fake girl who looks like Kate Winslet now?"

"NO!" I protested. "I'm sorry, but did you or did you not just see me being incinerated like a Duraflame log? Huh? Did you? Did you or did you not see my simulated face crying out for help as my skinny, thin, and perfectly toned arms tried to beat at the flames that were licking my body, which looked like to me was probably a size six? I finally had inner thighs that had never rubbed together, they had never even once touched, and now they are gone! That is a tragedy nearly unparalleled!"

And then I clicked the urn numerous additional times to emphasize my point.

It was right about that time that my husband stood up, leaned in closer to the screen, and pointed again.

"What IS THAT? What is that thing right near the fireman's foot in the front yard? Oh my God. *Oh my God.* What . . . what *have you done?!!*"

"It's just a turkey leg, you leave them all over the place," I let him know, and then went back to my keyboard for more clicks on the urn. "I'm going to make you cry until you're dehydrat—"

And then I saw what my husband saw. A big, spreading puddle right at the tip of the fireman's boot.

"Oh dear Lord," I commented quietly as my hand covered my mouth in shock.

"I hope you're happy!" my husband yelled. "*I hope you are happy.* LOOK AT THAT. I've peed my pants!! I've wet myself in front of a fireman!"

"Yes," I agreed. "Yes, you certainly have."

"HOO HOO HOOOO!" Laurie's Husband continued to cry as pee-pee ran down his leg and pooled in the front yard, and left a big, round dark spot on the front of his jeans.

"You were so busy making me cry and mourning you that you didn't bother to notice that my bladder needs were at alarming levels!" my husband scolded me.

"Well, it's not my fault. Maybe if you realized you had to tinkle when I was a bonfire," I replied, "I might still be alive!"

"Actually, now that I'm thinking about it, I do need to use the rest room," my husband said. "And all of that mourning has made me hungry! What are we making for dinner?"

"Oh," I said as I shook my head. "Not on your life!"

The Attack of BeanieQueenie

I've always been the mean sister.

Always.

In my family, there's the nice sister, the sensitive sister, and then me. In my role as the oldest child, I believe I have the right to be a little resentful, since my territory has been invaded not once, but twice.

So when the sensitive sister—or "BeanieQueenie," as she's known to the cyber world as an homage to her love for Beanie Babies—left for Flagstaff earlier this summer to work on her master's degree, I was really good and answered all of her e-mails. In them, I even offered to bring her warmer clothing and told her how I was pretty sure I had seen Divine, Gertrude Stein, and the Venus of Willendorf naked at the gym.

Soon, however, her e-mails trickled off as she made friends with other students, and her phone calls became more infrequent. And then, two weeks ago, something odd happened.

She started e-mailing again. It was slow at first, maybe one every couple of days, then one every other day, then every day. Two every day. Three every day.

Every time I got a message from BeanieQueenie, I sighed and shook my head. I knew what it was.

It was all CRAP.

Crappy jokes. Crappy stories with crappy punch lines. Crappy good-luck totem poles. Crappy psychological tests that are supposed to determine your crappy personality by playing word-association games. I didn't even get a personal greeting anymore; instead it was, "What's the first thing that comes to mind when you think of the word 'coffee'?" to which I naturally answered, "Only if I've had a lot to drink," just to discover at the end of the message that "coffee" was supposed to represent my attitude about sex.

When the damage escalated to four messages in one day, I knew something had to be done and sought commiseration with my other, nicer sister.

"Yeah, I know," she said, also with a sigh. "BeanieQueenie has been sending all that stuff to me, too, but she's sending it to me at work *and* at home. I'm getting double crap. It took me forty minutes to download a picture of Tweety Bird that someone made with all *V*'s and *M*'s. Did she send you that personality test?"

"Oh yes, " I added. "According to Dr. BeanieQueenie, I'm frigid. I said 'only when I'm drunk' to 'coffee.' "

"I said 'Smells good, but tastes bad,' " my sister added. "Where is she getting all of this stuff from?"

"As far as I can tell," I mentioned, "she's being supplied by a user—or shall I say pusher—known as LadyDi. Apparently, she's BeanieQueenie's funnies connection."

"Did LadyDi also send her the one about how bad an egg's life sucks?" my sister asked. " 'Because you only get laid once.' "

" 'And the only girl that ever sits on you is your mom,' " I said. "BeanieQueenie is out of control. We can't handle this on our own. I think we need to seek professional help."

So I took a big breath and did what I had to do. I called my mom, who was dealing with e-mail problems of her own after she somehow meandered into a chat room a couple of weeks ago.

"I didn't do any chatting," she quickly assured me then. "I didn't like any of the chatters' names, they all sounded like prostitutes and truck drivers."

Nevertheless, she apparently didn't leave the chat room unnoticed, because later that day she began being barraged with illustrated mail from assorted porno sites.

"I didn't know what it was. It said 'Juicy Fruit' at the top, so I opened it," she explained. "I thought it was you trying to be funny. But what I saw was real sin, I tell you, real sin. People forget that God once destroyed the world because of that kind of sin, and they weren't even taking pictures of it then! What I saw would *blind* a holy person."

But I didn't even need to explain about the BeanieQueenie situation, because my mom was on that mailing list, too.

"Oh, I don't know why you two can't get along," my mother said. "Leave your sister alone. She is just sharing her joy with you!"

"Mom," I whined, "she's not sharing joy. She sent me something nasty about an egg."

"I thought that was funny," she replied. " 'You have to share a room with eleven guys!!' But I didn't understand the one about 'sitting' . . . "

"The thing is," I continued, "never once in, say, thirty years has she ever called me to tell me a joke. But put a 'forward' button in front of her and all of a sudden she becomes Lenny Bruce."

"Don't you say anything mean to her!" my mother warned. "She was born tender, not with a rawhide heart like you!"

"COFFEE!!" I shouted.

"Never had it until I got married," she replied before she hung up.

I didn't know what to do. I thought about calling my sensitive sister and telling her that if she didn't stop the e-mails, I would wreak havoc by going in her room while she was away and touching EVERY SINGLE THING. To a girl that has her clothes arranged by the color order of the rainbow, that spelled Years of Intensive Therapy. If that didn't work, I knew I could break her if I threatened to mutilate one Beanie Baby at a time by removing the protective tag cover with each crappy e-mail I got.

I made the call.

"Hello, BeanieQueenie?" I said into the phone. "It's Queenie-Meanie, and we need to talk about those e-mails."

"Aren't they funny!" My sister giggled. "Did you get the one about the egg? 'Five minutes to make one hard and two to make it soft!' You work so hard all the time to make other people laugh that I just wanted to put a smile on your face. I was imagining you laughing when I sent it and it made me so happy!"

"Oh" was all I could say as I felt my meanness level plummet.

Go on, say it! Say it! the cruel little voice inside me yelled. Tell her you're going to go for all of the retired Beanies first! Tell her you have Doodle the Rooster in your hand right NOW!

"I didn't get the egg one," I heard myself say. "Could you send it again?"

Fill 'er Up

When the paper I worked for was bought by a large chain that installed its own management, things changed. We had a new editor in chief, who watched me blow a zeppelin out of my nose during a meeting, which in turn resulted in a bevy of phone messages and e-mails submitting an apology regarding the booger bubble, and also requesting an additional audience, none of which he bothered replying to.

My direct editor for my once-a-week newspaper column was replaced as well, and Gretchen, a six-foot-three emaciated giantess with a shock of cropped black hair and a closetful of safari clothing (including a khaki bandanna around her neck), became my new editor.

Things went well, as long as you're counting the first five seconds of our working relationship, but after we said hello to each other, they fell apart rather quickly. Especially when Gretchen told me that she had noticed on the way to work, at the diagonal ends of an intersection, a man selling strawberries and another man selling piñatas.

And then she grinned oddly, as if she was waiting for me to say something.

"That's a wonderful slice of Phoenix, isn't it?" she said from behind her grin.

"I suppose if you've got a fruit hankering and a desire to release all of your underlying yet bubbling to the surface aggression by beating on a disfigured papier-mâché donkey, sure," I answered, since I thought she was joking.

"It was so colorful," she said, looking off into the distance. "That's what you should be writing about. That's what your column needs to be. Slices of Phoenix, the flavor of Phoenix."

I was stunned so badly that I couldn't even burst out into laughter. "It's funny you say that since you just moved here," I told her. "I've been here since 1972, and I've tasted Phoenix many times. The flavor is called 'dust.' Go out there with your mouth open. You'll taste it, too."

That's when Gretchen turned around in her cubicle, began typing something, and pretended that I wasn't there.

"Gretchen," I said, but she kept her back turned toward me. "I'm sorry. We're getting off on the wrong foot, and I really don't want that."

Nothing.

I called her a couple more times, but she acted like I had vanished. She completely ignored me.

So I decided that maybe I had been too harsh and that the best way to save my column was to give her hers. I came up with an idea to go and talk to the two vendors on her Slice of Phoenix corner, see if they knew each other, and try to find something humorous about it.

When I approached her cubicle the next day, she waved excitedly when she saw me and seemed nearly jubilant, and that's when I tried to ignore the fact that she was wearing a man's necktie and a fedora.

"Hi!" she said, leaning forward too give me a half hug.

"Hi!" I said, trying to return the happiness. "I thought about it all night, and I think I know how I can write a flavorful piece about the strawberries and piñatas!"

She looked as me as if I had just said, "Bigfoot is in my office with the Loch Ness Monster and the Chupacabra! Wanna see?"

"Why would you do that?" she asked, her brow furrowing. "Who told you to do that?"

"You did," I replied.

"That is ridiculous!" she stormed. "Why would I want a story about a man selling strawberries? That's, that's just ludicrous and how dare you say that I would suggest such a thing, because I wouldn't. I wouldn't. That is a stupid idea!"

Then she turned around again and pretended I wasn't there.

I really didn't know what to do, so I kept writing the same column I always did and submitting it to Gretchen, who would wield her editing skills like a blind, arthritic surgeon. She helped herself to amputating punch lines, rewriting jokes, and eliminating various people in my column, often rendering it senseless and unrelatable to the accompanying illustration. She barely remembered our conversations, often denied that we had agreed on a column idea, and on occasion would call my extension and say, "Who *is* this?"

Over the next several months, I came to realize that there was a high possibility that Gretchen had tenants. In her body. Now I'm not sure which one the "host Gretchen" was, and I honestly didn't care, but there were four distinct facets of my editor; there was the Ernest Hemingway Gretchen, who basically came to work dressed for a lion hunt in Kenya minus the gun and who would wax poetic about her observations about the paper towel dispenser in the bathroom or the vending machine in the cafeteria; there was the Annie Hall Gretchen, who came to work in the apparel of James Cagney and overanalyzed every story idea as if she were passing a bill in Congress; then there was Madame-the-Puppet Gretchen, when she would show up to work in what frightfully looked like opera makeup and enabled anyone to lip-read her ranting from an amazing two blocks; but the nastiest Gretchen was Scary, Indigent Gretchen, who would come to the office with stringy hair and a distinct scent reminiscent of a person who hasn't had access to running water for numerous consecutive days and had a tendency to rant to no one in particular that everyone was trying to attack her. Madame looked like Heidi Klum in comparison.

Honestly, once I figured out that my editor was Sybil, I had some sympathy for her, I really did. But between Scary, Indigent Gretchen moving my column to different sections of the paper every other week, with Annie Hall Gretchen taking a machete to my column and hacking it like a side of pork, and with Ernest Hemingway Gretchen insisting that I needed to write about the ambiguous relationship between the cactus wren and the saguaro or a personal reflection about the perfection of a brown-bubbled tortilla, I was seriously losing my shit. Madame Gretchen wasn't that mean, she was just uneasy to look at, but it did make spotting Gretchen way across the newsroom in a group of men a piece of cake, and therefore easy to escape from. My job as a columnist had been perfect until now, it had been flawless, and I couldn't figure out what was happening or how to fix it. While it was too bad that Gretchen was the Three Thousand Faces of Eve, it also wasn't my case study to solve. I had my own problems in simply dealing with her, and frankly, I was afraid that she was pushing me to the point where I was going to need to develop some of my own auxiliary personalities as a psychological defense mechanism. I was already having nightmares that I had shown up to work in a pith helmet myself, holding a spear and speaking in a British accent.

Then an odd thing happened. Instead of recognizing Gretchen as the feral, unpredictable, easily spooked editor with the *Memento*-like memory that she was and addressing the problem, the new editor in chief did something else entirely.

He promoted her.

While I was reeling from this news, trying anything to prevent Gretchen from out-and-out ruining my career, another odd thing happened. People on Gretchen's staff—editors that had been with the paper for fifteen, twenty years, began to quit, asked to be transferred to a different section, applied for other jobs, and just plain refused to work with her.

When Gretchen allegedly e-mailed several editors and threatened to come to their houses and beat them up, she was demoted and given the odd title of "writing coach," demoted again, given the title of "headline chief," demoted again, and finally deported to a satellite office somewhere in newspaper Siberia.

A metaphorical house had fallen on her. All of the shortest people in the department got together and danced a symbolic jig. The skies cleared. A rainbow appeared. Things were looking up.

My new editor, Suzzi, who had just returned from maternity leave after giving birth to twins, took over Gretchen's spot. I was relieved, exhilarated, hopeful. I wanted to hug her. I wanted to love her.

Our first meeting went well, in comparison with my introduction to Gretchen. Suzzi showed me photos of her orange-haired twin girls, who looked . . . "happy," I said. "They're so . . . happy!"

"Being a mother of twins has given me a whole new perspective on this department," she commented. "Being a mother of twins is an exceptional experience. It really opens you up to all intellectual levels. Becoming a parent raises you to a level that people with no children really can't reach."

I didn't know what to say to that, so I smiled and nodded.

"I haven't lost the baby weight, but I will, I will," Suzzi assured me. "I mean, I had twins, you know? Twice the baby, twice the weight!"

I nodded some more, although I wanted to give her a little tip that if she was so concerned about her weight, wearing a tight-fitting, baby-style, size P Abercrombie & Fitch tee wasn't the best look for her, especially since the hem had rolled upward due to its incapacity to deal with her expanse, and was now informing me what twin-size stretch marks looked like.

"So, I will be editing your column, and I think we can take it in many new and exciting directions," she said. "You have kids, don't you? I think that would be a great direction for you."

"Oh," I stuttered. "No, no, I don't have kids."

"But I thought you were married?" Suzzi said, looking quite confused. On her next exhale, her T-shirt rolled up another inch.

"Well, I am married, but my husband is concentrating on school, I work long hours here, and now isn't the right time," I tried to explain. "My first book is coming out in a couple of months, and I'm focusing on that, too."

"Is there ever a right time?" Suzzi said softly. "I had TWINS. When is there a right time for twins? But I'm a mother of two, and having two gives me twice the awareness than just having one. The awareness is incredible. I'm so much smarter."

"Well, okay," I said, trying to draw an unsettling conversation to a close. "I'll have my new column done tomorrow, and I'll e-mail it over."

"Oh, sure," Suzzi said with a smile.

And I did. It was a piece about a new campaign in Phoenix that was intended to prevent red-light running, although the strategy consisted of placing mammoth signs above the streets that would scream out DON'T!!; the next sign, about a hundred feet farther down the road, would yell RUN!!; the next one RED!!; and the next one LIGHTS!! in a Burma Shave fashion. Now in my opinion, I simply stated, if a campaign was going to be effective, it should emphasize keeping the drivers' eyes on the road and on traffic signals instead of everywhere *but* the road, while trying to solve the word puzzle shrieking at them from the sky.

Ten minutes after I e-mailed the column to Suzzi, I received a reply from my new, doubly aware editor who strongly insisted that I mention in my column the number of people killed every year as a result of red-light running.

I took a deep breath, and I felt my face get hot. I had just spent months under the rule of Gretchen, and this situation didn't have the initial earmarks of anything better. She wanted me to insert the dead into my column. I simply did not know how to pull that off. How do you make tragic deaths fit into a humor column? I couldn't. Even the Annie Hall Gretchen would have understood that. "I can't make senseless deaths funny," I tried to tell Suzzi in my e-mail reply. "Corpses tend to be a bit of a bummer. Throw one into a party, and you'll see what I mean. Typically, they don't liven things up, so to speak."

I wasn't trying to be snotty—well, maybe a little, I was; actually, yes, I was trying to be very snotty since at that moment I was completely unable to control myself. I wanted to be as snotty as possible, which I will agree was not the mature, appropriate response.

But I was trying to make a point, especially since Suzzi had completely missed the one in my column.

In the end, it didn't matter.

Several days later, I had a hint that something bad was coming when another editor told me that Suzzi had said to her, "Would it be the end of the world if we stopped running Laurie's column?" And sure enough, within twenty-four hours, Suzzi rolled down the hall in another revealing knit shirt and found my office. She parked herself in a chair opposite mine.

"Hi," she said. "How are you?"

"I think I'm about to find out," I said, looking at her.

"Last week's column will be your final one," she said as she tilted her head. "They don't really fit what we currently need."

"Why?" I asked, as suddenly her torso simply produced another fat roll and it popped out like an escalator stair, obviously forced upward by a pair of too tight pants, an experience I knew all too well. No more room in the pen.

"Because," she simply offered.

"And that's it?" I said, questioning her. "I don't get to say goodbye to any of the readers that have been following the column for ten years? You're just going to pull it? You're going to kill me off like I was on a soap opera?"

She shrugged and smiled.

"Well, I have to let you know that if you don't provide me an opportunity for a last column to at least explain, I'll have to tell my readers another way," I told her point-blank. "I have an extensive e-mail list."

"Well, then," she said in a saccharine voice, "maybe if you start an e-mail campaign, you can get your little column back."

"That's fine by me," I said, looking her straight in the eye. "And you are aware that I have a book coming out in a matter of months?"

"You know," Suzzi said as she stood up, although her brand-new fat roll just stayed where it was. "if I see you on the *Today* show, I guess I'll know that I've made a mistake."

And with that, she walked out of my office and that was it. My column was gone. That's cool, I thought to myself as I tried really, really hard not to freak out, you have it your way, Suzzi. And I'll have it mine. What the hell do you know, anyway? You don't even know that you gave birth to orangutans. Carrot babies. You had carrot babies! And not just one, *two*!! It was like you popped out a Birds Eye frozen vegetable pack. Honestly, I was tired. I was really, really tired. I was exhausted. I had fought for my column really hard ever since Gretchen showed up. And frankly, I would have rather let my column go than let someone ruin it.

The following Wednesday night, true to my word, I wrote an e-mail to the readers I had received letters from, explaining that my column had been killed, and it wouldn't be in the paper the next day. I thanked them for sticking by me for so long, and that it had been a great run.

Additionally, I wrote, if they wanted to e-mail someone about the cancellation, they sure could.

And then I put two cherries on my e-mail sundae in the form of the Big Cheese Editor's and Suzzi's e-mail addresses.

Send. Click.

I mailed it off.

The next morning, when Suzzi and the Big Cheese editor came to work , sat down at their desks, and checked to see if they had mail, they did indeed.

They had so much mail it clogged their e-mail boxes, and I heard that it took several support techs a while to fix it, because about one thousand messages arrived overnight and they just kept coming throughout that day, the next day, and the next.

After all, Suzzi had challenged me. I just met her on it.

I never got my column back. But I think it was safe to say that one, at the very least, of my needs had been filled.

It's Alive!!!!!

As I looked at the letter in my hand from the City of Phoenix that I received several weeks ago, my blood began to bubble. It explained that a complaint had been filed against my front yard, claiming that it contained an inordinate amount of trash and overgrown weeds.

With my hands shaking, I wondered out loud if this was a joke. While it's plainly obvious that my landscape will never appear on the cover of *House & Garden*, the City of Phoenix had to be kidding. Maybe we didn't mow as often as we should, but rest assured a small child never got lost in the grass, nor had anyone mistaken it for a cornfield. That was at my old house.

When we bought our house, it had been vacant for two years. The yard was a dirt parking lot, and virtually every one of the sixteen trees on the property were brown, cracked, and dead. Eventually, we pulled most of them out, with the exception of an ancient orange tree that escaped the chain saw. It had one green branch that made my husband insist that the tree was still alive, but it also survived because the ax was stolen before we got to that side of the yard. Since then, I've requested a chain saw at every birthday and Christmas to take the tree down, but until I got a note from my old therapist, no one would let me have one.

On a hunch, I sought out all of my neighbors, and discovered, not to my surprise, that we had all received the same letter on the same day. There could be only one culprit, I decided, as I shot an evil eye toward his house. It had to be the Neighborhood Nemesis, or, as he likes to call himself, the president of the neighborhood association—a man who doesn't even have a yard, only a small strip of grass as wide as my thigh. I once attended an association meeting, but when Neighborhood Nemesis proudly boasted that he spent the majority of his nights running up and down his street armed with a video camera taping his neighbors, I became too freaked out to go anymore. The letter was plainly the result of his walking up and down my street, writing down what he didn't like, and then calling the city to rat us out.

I was loading the eggs and a big slingshot into the car when my husband came home from work.

"Look at this!" I yelled as I waved the letter in front of him.

"What are you doing with all of those eggs, honey?" my husband said slowly. "If you bought chickens from our neighbors, I'm going to be mad!"

"No chickens," I said smugly, handing over the complaint. "I'm gonna catch myself a rat!"

"There's nothing wrong with our yard!" my husband yelled as he read the letter and then pointed: "That tree is ALIVE!!!" I haven't seen him that mad since a bartender carded him, laughed, and said, "Does your sister know you have her license?"

We jumped in my car to drive to the Nemesis's house and launch our attack, but there he was, standing out in his front strip, taping stuff. I stumbled for an insult to yell, but all I managed to say was, "It's ALIVE!!!!!" Then we went home and had omelets for dinner.

The next day, I was eating an egg salad sandwich when someone knocked on my door, a raggedy man who asked if I needed any yard work done. I smiled as if God had sent him there Himself. It had to be a sign.

I motioned toward the orange tree.

"Fifty bucks," he said through the gap where his teeth used to be.

"Can you knock it down before my husband comes home?" I asked.

Before I knew it, the man, whose name was Jerry, took a running start and jumped on the tree, breaking off massive branches with his bare hands. I went back inside, too afraid that I'd be called as a witness in a lawsuit against me after Jerry had impaled himself on a twig. With every loud "SNAP!" that I heard from within my office, I got more and more frightened.

What kind of guy does yard work for a living . . . without tools? I wondered. Where were his teeth? Who breaks apart a tree with his hands? Through the window, I peeked outside, and that's when I saw two of them, Jerry and his "assistant," violently swinging on the tree like monkeys as they rocked it back and forth. Then they landed and kicked it until it was dead.

I sat down and wrote a note in case the FBI might need it once my husband spotted the freshly opened and still somewhat flexible bounty of chocolate Twizzlers in the cabinet, proof positive that if my favorite snack was present without one or both of my hands in it, there had to be some sort of foul play involved.

"I have two homeless guys trying to kick down the dead orange tree in our front yard," I typed. "I'm going to describe them to you so if they end up robbing and killing me, you can give the police a lead once you realize months from now that I am gone and not just on a diet: Guy #1, 'Jerry': No teeth. Short. Possibly going through withdrawal of some kind. Guy #2: 'Assistant': Some teeth. Shorter. Apparent aggression issues. Oh. Now there's one less tooth. And it just may be lodged in one of suspect #1's knuckles."

I ran outside to access the damage. "That's very nice," I nodded at Jerry, who was emphatically grinning and nodding back. "Now you have to leave before my husband comes home. Here's some eggs."

Within seconds, my husband's truck pulled up in front of the house. He got out slowly, glared at me, and then walked inside without saying a word.

"The tree is gone!" I said excitedly with a big smile.

"No, I wouldn't say that," he answered. "The tree is not gone. It's lying in five hundred pieces around the yard. Who are those guys?

Why are you talking to strangers when you're in the house alone? Who told you to mutilate the tree? You've ruined everything!"

"There were only four green leaves left on that tree," I said quietly. "I was pretty sure that a comeback was out of the question."

"That's not it!" my husband yelled. "Now I have to take back your Christmas present!"

I gasped with glee. "But the therapist wouldn't write the note when I asked her," I said, jumping up and down.

"It's okay," my husband said, shuffling toward his study. "I bought an electric-powered chain saw with a plug-in cord so if I run away fast enough, you can only chase me so far."

"There's a tree in the backyard with only six green leaves on it," I suggested.

"It's ALIVE!" my husband shot back.

The Haunting of Jerry

Someone' s knocking at my door. I have a feeling it's Jerry.

I almost liked Jerry when he first came to my house and pulled out the semidead orange tree from my front yard, using nothing but his bare hands and a whole lot of angst. I was amazed as he rocked the tree out of its earthen bed with his homeless little man-child body, exposing the tree roots and leaving a crater big enough to barbecue a hog in.

I liked him as he unabashedly gave me a tour of his battle scars, showing me a six-inch former wound on his head that he sustained while wrestling with the private parts of a particularly mean queen palm, the way he could flip his arm around like a rag doll after he dislocated his shoulder after a forty-foot tumble, and the way he had to close one eye in order to make the right cut on a tree, and not the imaginary one.

He was proud of his work, and pointed to various palm trees in the neighborhood, claiming that the bulbous, circular necks under the fronds were his "signature," though in my opinion, they looked a little more like goiters than a trademark.

"No matter how many times I've fallen out of a tree," he boasted, "I've never sued anybody. I'll sign anything you got."

He must have told the same thing to my next-door neighbor. After he finished killing my orange tree, he scurried up a fifty-year-old palm in her backyard like a squirrel in the dead of night, and left his signature with a saw and only the stars to guide him.

My husband, however, was not as impressed with Jerry as I was.

"You are not allowed to answer the door anymore," he said simply and firmly.

"Come on," I said. "The man weighs eighty pounds and can only see straight if he covers one eye! I could knock him over with a fart. Besides, I assessed the situation and decided that he was harmless. He won't sue us, he said he'd sign anything."

"A serial killer will always try to gain your trust!" he replied. "What good is a lawsuit after he's eaten your brain like it was chili?"

I was getting my morning coffee the next day when I looked up and gasped. From my kitchen window I saw Jerry, again forty feet up in the air, hugging my other neighbor's palm tree with one hand while he waved to me with the other. It was a very friendly gesture, although you are never really ready for a homeless tree trimmer to extend a greeting to you from the sky when you're not wearing a bra or pants.

For about a week after that, Jerry came by every day to see if I needed any more work done. I kept saying no, mostly because I felt I was lucky that Jerry hadn't already dismembered himself or accidentally fallen on some electrical wires on my property. His physical disfigurements didn't bother me as much as my suspicion that he had a hankering for hooch, and was tanked a fair amount of the time. The last thing I really needed was a television news crew parked in my backyard, filming a fireman relentlessly poking at Jerry's hot, pickled body with a stick until he fell headfirst into the waiting recycling bin.

Finally, however, Jerry wore me down, especially when he began showing up at night, wanting to cut something up. To get rid of him, I agreed that he could cut the shortest tree—one that really wouldn't have presented much of a challenge to a three-year-old armed with a dull butter knife—on one condition. He had to start work early in the morning, so he would be somewhat sober, thus significantly reducing the risk of death, injury, or loss of electrical power to my house, because I really hate resetting clocks.

Jerry went to work, and scampered up the tree in someone's old golf shoes and a harness made out of a retired motorcycle chain and a bunch of frayed rope. I spent the next hour searching my homeowner's policy for a homeless, drunk tree-trimmer clause until Jerry knocked on the door and said that his signature was done and he was thirsty.

With a sigh of relief, I paid him more than the tree was worth, gave him the last can of Mountain Dew, and said good-bye.

"Now you have done it," my husband said to me as I closed the front door. "You've fed him. That's like leaving a whole ham on a picnic table in bear country. You'll never get rid of him, and he'll probably start breeding in the crawl space under our house!"

He was right. In fact, Jerry came back every time he got a little hungry, every time he got a little thirsty, and every time he ran out of cigarettes. Then he said that I had been so nice to him that he'd trim my palm trees next year for $30, which was a deal.

"Thank you, Jerry," I said, agreeing to the deal. "That's very nice."

"Can I have half of it now?" he asked.

Apparently, I was Jerry's gold mine, and though he eventually stopped asking for work, he just started asking me for outright cash. When he popped up on my porch at ten o'clock on a Sunday night, I had had it. I solely bore the responsibility of creating my own human feral cat.

"I need twenty dollars," Jerry said as I opened the door. "Consider it a loan."

"Jerry," I said harshly, "I'm a writer. We eat ramen four nights a week and ramen bake the other three!"

"Fifteen!"

"No," I answered.

"Ten! I'll take ten!"

"Jerry!" I yelled as loud as I could. "The bank is bust!"

As I closed the door, I felt really bad for him. I kept on feeling really bad about it until my husband did the math, figured out that in the two days that Jerry had done work for us and our neighbors, he had made more than we both did in a week. In fact, it turned out, Jerry was making himself a pretty healthy salary.

"TAX-FREE," my husband said, adding insult to injury.

"Now that I think about it," I said, turning things over in my mind, "he always wore clean clothes. And I've never seen him wear the same thing twice."

"Do you think it's a scam?" my husband asked.

I didn't know; I still don't. I do know that Jerry keeps himself pretty busy. I've seen him almost every day, fifty feet up in the air, hacking away at someone's tree, dangerously close to the power lines. I see him, but I don't wave anymore.

And right now, I can hear him knocking, but he can't come in.

FIRE! FIRE! FIRE!

It wouldn't be at all unusual for someone to be banging on my front door at 3 A.M. on a Tuesday morning.

And that's exactly what I was thinking as I shuffled to the door amid the panicked, frenzied, "stranger danger" barks of my dog. It wouldn't be at all unusual. I've opened the door at more inappropriate times to find a variety of characters on the other side. After all, I'm not living in Scottsdale or Paradise Valley, where Stevie Nicks lives, high on a mountain—I just had to be an urban girl, be in the middle of things and buy a house with character—which just happens to be down the street from a newly opened casket store. Now, I know what you're thinking, but it's not a mortuary—it's a casket store, for those DIY burial sort of people. Buryin' on a budget. The store just sells caskets. Nothing else. Caskets. In fact, the store isn't even called something pretty like the Casket Basket or Eternal Slumber. The sign just says CASKETS. What kind of neighborhood has a casket store, you ask? Well, not a very nice one, I'll tell you.

Now, because of the kind of area I live in, my door-knocker could very well be Jerry. I thought it was odd that Jerry's brand of horticulture was ripping the former orange tree apart limb by limb with his hands and kicking it down with kung fu moves until I understood that Jerry was no horticulturist but just your average, run-of-the-mill Apache Junction tweaker with battery acid and lye shooting through his bloodstream and not a dime to his name. Jerry, alarmingly, had taken a particular fancy to me, and to this day, when he's not incarcerated, he pops up on my front porch during all hours of the day and night, demanding money, cigarettes, or Mountain Dew.

Or my door-knocker could be the guy who pointed to a house across the street, introduced himself as my neighbor, and asked my husband for money because he needed to "buy medication for his pregnant wife." Finding it unlikely that Rebecca, the woman who lives in the house across the street, was pregnant by this guy since I'd seen her the day before riding a motorcycle manned by her girlfriend, Jane, I advised the fictitious father-to-be, "Next time, don't point out a house with a rainbow flag waving from the porch."

Or my door-knocker could be the guy who looked like a high school senior and went door-to-door armed with a photograph of a little girl, claiming that the child was his recently departed daughter and he needed money to bury her, despite the fact that the aged, yellowed, circa 1970s Polaroid was older than he was. Smelling suspicion because the words "car wash" were not even used once (the typical method for people in my neighborhood to raise the necessary funds to bury the remains of their loved ones) and he didn't know how his "baby girl" had died and also didn't know her name, I declined to make a donation to help bury a fake kid and told him that if he relayed his story to the casket store down the street, maybe he could cut himself a deal.

So, honestly, when I answered the door that night, I wasn't particularly worried about who was on the other side; I just wanted him or her to go away and let my Tylenol PM do the work God intended it to do. And sure enough, as soon as I opened that door, there stood some woman I had never seen before, hardly clothed, hair all tousled, and barefoot, who claimed she was my neighbor and then screamed, "Fire! Fire! Fire! Your backyard is on fire!"

"Let's make a deal—I'll give you my last can of Mountain Dew and some cigarette butts if you promise to go smoke that crack pipe of yours in someone else's front yard," I almost said, but instead, my eyes followed her pointed finger, which was directed to my dining room windows that faced the backyard.

And that was when I saw fire.

Fire in the backyard that we had just begun to landscape, after seven years during which it was a barren plot of dirt and could have easily been mistaken for Oklahoma, 1935. This time, I had veered away from crystal meth addicts and had hired real landscapers to tear down the three dead orange trees, install a sprinkler system, and put down sod, which had just been delivered that afternoon and was still resting on pallets that I thought were surely now a big ball of flame.

I am here to tell you that nothing will frighten you more than an inferno quickly eating its way toward your house, and I've come home after the DEA ransacked my house and went through my underwear drawer, so I know fear when I see it.

"Fire! Fire! Fire!" I screamed to my husband, who was still resting soundly while our home was about to be reduced to kindling. "My sod is on fire!

"Get up! Call 911!" I shrieked as I threw the phone at him and then ran into the backyard.

I wasn't exactly sure what to do; I mean, I was rather freaked out. I wasn't at all prepared for a fire. In fact, I had pretty much figured that my chances of encountering one essentially became nonexistent when I quit smoking and drinking at the same time. The only thing I knew to do in case of a fire was drop and roll, and in this case, I thought the drop-and-roll maneuver was a wee bit premature since I wasn't on fire yet (although I was not ruling out the possibility), plus, if anyone saw me, I'd look kinda stupid. So I did the only thing I knew to do, which was to grab the garden hose and pray to God that it was still intact, since we use it so infrequently it was a miracle that it hadn't shriveled up to the size of a shoelace. I turned it on and ran to the back fence, where the fire was roaring, thankfully, not in my backyard, but in the alley behind the fence, where the remnants of the three dead orange trees were placed.

Directed by my shoeless, anonymous neighbor who was now

standing on the alley side of the fence, I lifted the hose over the wall and ran the trickle over the hottest spots. Apparently, something of a crowd had begun to gather on the other side of the wall to watch my decrepit hose spit on the blaze, although none of my neighbors ran back and forth with additional hoses, pails, or bowls of water as I would have imagined they would after seeing fires run rampant on *Little House on the Prairie.* No, nobody made a move to start a bucket brigade or anything like that to save my house from catching fire, they just stood and watched, chatted cordially among themselves like they were at a block party, when suddenly I heard someone say, "Did anyone call the fire department?" and my blood ran cold.

The fire department.

Goddamn it! I said to myself. See, that is exactly what you get. Goddamn it! Exactly what you get for violating your own set of rules you invented and vowed to live by when you were in eighth grade, which includes #1: Never date a guy who drives a Camaro, Trans Am, or has any type of "car art" performed on his vehicle, particularly if it involves a horny Viking maiden wielding a sword, wearing a metal bra, and who has a snake wrapped around her leg, hissing; #2: When you get married, arise an extra hour early to curl hair and apply makeup and then go back to bed so your husband never sees you ugly and thinks that you wake up beautiful; and #3: Always go to bed with curled hair and a full face of makeup because you never know when you might encounter a hot, foxy, and perhaps shirtless fireman.

And look at you now! Not a stitch of concealer, no mascara, not even lip liner. This is your one chance to encounter a fireman and here you are, just a hag with a hose. That's what they're going to call you, you know. Hose Hag. Why could you just not adhere to the rules? Why? Just once follow the rules!

Right then, I heard the wail of sirens and another thought hit me, like a bolt of lightning. "To hell with the makeup," a big, deep voice in my head declared. "Because you're not wearing pants."

I gasped. I looked down. It was true. I wasn't wearing pants. I had been fighting this fire, in its entirety, in my underwear and a tank top that provided no support for my sandbag boobs and no hidden sanctuary for the flesh curtains that are my upper arms.

"Honey!" I heard my husband scream as he ran toward me. "The police are here! The police are here and you're only wearing panties!"

I turned around and handed the hose off to my husband, who then looked at me quizzically and said, "Why do you look much better when I wake up in the morning?"

No New People

Frankly, I had never been happier to see a half-naked lesbian in all my life. In fact, there were four hundred of them, topless, bouncing, shouting, and heading my way.

I was absolutely thrilled.

I was on vacation with my friends Michelle and Maxie, and we had come up to San Francisco for several days to get out of the heat of the Phoenix summer. Maxie had looked up a friend of hers, Paula, who lived in the area, and suggested that we all meet for dinner so she could give us tips for what we should do for the rest of our trip.

I'm not big on meeting new people, especially new people I'm never going to see again. There's all kinds of uninteresting, insincere banter, I have to pretend to be a nice person, and because 96 percent of the world's population are dim bulbs, odds are excellent that I'll be stuck in the middle of a Spontaneous Freak Encounter. For Maxie, though, I was willing to make an exception to my "No New People" rule. I was going to open my soggy, rotten tomato heart and try to like the new person.

Enter Paula: Identified by enough yardage of purple gauze to build a mess tent above the waist and sporting what looked like Princess Jasmine harem pants below, Paula resembled someone who bought out a Pier 1 clearance clothing sale in 1988 and never looked back. The ensemble, as a whole, cried "tragedy" as well as

"I can make my own soap." I'm not exactly sure I can describe her tresses, except to say that they had a Bon Jovi air about them and said, "That's what happens when you think you're pretty good at cutting your own hair." I was far too terrified to look at her feet, because I do believe I'd caught a glimpse of something sparkly in addition to an elfinlike point. And then, I saw it. The ultimate bad omen, worse than spotting a "666" birthmark on the back of someone's neck. A THUMB ring. Oh yes. Paula was a proud and active New Ager, and the first thing that popped into my head as I absorbed her Paulaness was, "This one excessively uses the word 'goddess' and her bathroom is covered in framed angel posters."

But that's not all, because Paula was bearing another accessory; her small, meek, and socially paralyzed sister, Wendy.

That's right. TWO new people.

From a distance, Wendy looked reasonably regular, and she wasn't dressed as if she were moments away from casting a spell. But the expression on her face was something quite different, as if her sister were taking her to meet a coven of witches, something I'd bet cold, hard cash had happened before. And I'd double those odds that they were all wearing pointy, sparkly shoes.

As soon as we sat down at the restaurant, Paula flagged down the waitress and ordered a Vanilla Stoli, Diet Coke, and cherry concoction, while the rest of us ordered iced tea. That's not very New Age, I thought, cringing, that's just *gross.* Shouldn't there be some chai or tabouli in that drink? But whatever. I'm not here to judge, I reminded myself, I'm just here to witness the freak show that's minutes away from starting.

"Paula, you look a little stressed for a girl who's in love," Maxie mentioned with a sly smile. "Tell us about this new guy you've been seeing."

Ooooo, goody! I cooed to myself, New Age *amore*! I bet she reeled him in with the smoke of patchouli, incantations to the Earth Mother, and a sprinkle of fairy dust! I scooted my chair closer, anxious to find out if her beau was a bead artist, bamboo flute player, or better yet, a space traveler!

"Well," Paula started, her facial expression shooting off sparks of anger, "maybe we weren't so right for each other after all."

Maxie reached for Paula's hand in sympathy.

"He said we were moving too fast," Paula said and heavily sighed as the waitress placed the Vanilla Stoli/Diet Coke aberration before her. "You know, my heart didn't come with a speedometer, I told him! When you're flying on the wings of love, is there really a speed limit? And he even once agreed that our sexual energy had elements of art in it."

"Boy," I was aching to say, "during the cleanup, I bet the paint thinner was brutal."

"I'm so sorry—" Maxie started.

"You know, I really don't want to talk about him," Paula suddenly snapped before she took several gulps from her cocktail and the table grew quiet.

"I had a stroke," Wendy offered.

"You mean you had four," her sister Paula finished as the ice in her glass clinked together. "Waitress! I need another Vanilla Stoli and Diet Coke with a cherry!"

"I had four strokes," Wendy said with a smile.

"Maxie, I'm going to this new church, and I LOVE it!" Paula exclaimed. "Only women are allowed in the temple, and you can go there to bathe in this communal bath, it's an incredible sharing experience. So I'm glad only women are permitted because I can't stand the sight of a man right now."

"I'm so sorry—" Maxie tried.

"You know, I really don't want to talk about him," Paula said sharply, taking a healthy chug from her new drink. "I'm seeing a new hypnotherapist, and she is so wise and warm, she's very celestial. She has golden hair that flows around her head like a halo. And honestly, I don't think"— Paula paused for dramatic effect before delivering what rolled in as my favorite proclamation of the evening—"*she's human*! Waitress! I need another drink! With a cherry!"

I'll take "Goddess" for two hundred, Alex, my mind screamed.

"She's just a goddess, either that or an ET," Paula went on.

"Extraterrestrial. She has that quality that so many of them have, so light and airy."

Could she be Flaky, goddess of croissants? I silently questioned myself.

"My husband left me," Wendy chirped.

"She's working me through regression to try and survive the abandonment of my lover," Paula finished.

"I'm so sorry—" Maxie said.

"You know, I really don't want to talk about him," Paula spit out, going to work on her fresh beverage. "It was at this very table that he looked into my eyes and told me we had traveled together before in past lives."

"I lost my job when one side of my mouth froze," Wendy said.

"And over there, at that table," Paula warbled as she pointed, "was where he said he could see my soul through my eyes. And over there," Paula said as she pointed toward the entrance, "is the door he opened for me on our first date. Our first date, only a short, two weeks ago. It seems like a life . . . time."

Well, it is, for a housefly! my brain sang, but I didn't say it. Instead, I looked at Michelle across the table and mouthed, "I can't believe we didn't have to pay for this show!"

"Are you ready to order?" the waitress asked.

"Vanilla Coke and Diet Stoli!" Paula cried out with a slur. "And the sherry! I need the sherry!"

"We'll just take the check—er, the bar tab, please," I said. "And the biggest barf bag you have."

Walking back to the hotel, Paula pointed out all the areas of interest. To her.

"See that sidewalk? We stepped on that on the way to his car.

"See that parking meter? That's where we parked.

"See this air? I bet some of it was in his lungs!"

Paula was pointing to a flattened piece of gum on the street that she was pretty sure was once in her ex-boyfriend's mouth when suddenly, four hundred topless lesbians and their eight hundred bobbing, flopping, and swinging tatas turned the corner and marched our way in the beginning of a Gay Pride parade. We watched the girls pass as they shouted, cheered, and walked along. I, for one, was not going to pass up a sight like that; it was like a *National Geographic* photo had sprung to life. I stood and gawked like the tourist I was, noticing at the same time that most of those knockers hadn't seen a bra since middle school. A little support goes a long way, I noted to myself, because once your chi-chis fall, man, they're down for the count. There's no rebounding when your opponent is gravity.

Paula, for the first time that evening, did not say a word. She stood slack-jawed as the parade passed, and due to her blood alcohol level, I'm sure she probably saw twice as many naked sisters as we did.

"I wonder if Paula sees any faces she recognizes?" I said to Michelle. "I'm sure she's shared dirty bathwater with at least a handful of those goddesses!"

"Who's looking at faces?" Michelle replied. "All I know is that I'm never taking my bra off again."

When the parade had passed and the shouts were starting to fade, it was Wendy who spoke first.

"Thank you so much for such a wonderful night!" she said with a wide smile, shaking our hands. "It was so nice to meet you. You are so kind to listen to someone else's problems like that. You know, I haven't spoken that much to anyone in months! It felt so good to get it all off my chest!"

"Well, it was our pleasure," I said, and then leaned forward. "But the next time your sister starts on her Anna Nicole Smith impression, make her eat a piece of bread first. That way, she can postpone prying used gum off the sidewalk for a couple of drinks."

"Well," Wendy giggled. "I'm hoping for a quiet drive home!"

"Your sister is so loaded that an aspirin would put her under. It was nice to meet you," I said to her, and I really meant it. "Here's my last Tylenol, and keep that bag handy!"

"Wow," Paula said, shaking her head. "I think I just channeled a vision of ancient Amazon women warriors marching into battle! I think they transcended time and space to send me a message!"

"Best of luck deciphering that message, because," I said, then paused for dramatic effect, *"I don't think they were human!"*

I Love Everybody

I was about to do a bad, bad thing.

I knew it. I just couldn't help it. As soon as I saw that big fat hand reach up and grab the last two chocolate chip cookie nuggets from the sample tray, I knew it was my signal. I was going in for the kill.

I'm a bad girl.

And I can prove it.

Earlier that morning, I had seen that very thing posted on a website.

"With undistinguished prose, leaden humor, insistent self-deprecation, almost zero detail about anything other than the state of her immediate surroundings," the review from *Kirkus*—an organization dedicated solely to publishing anonymous book reviews that mostly serve to expose books' endings—said, "the author succeeds in making herself and her circle appear purely unappealing."

Wow, I thought. That's bad. That is one bad review. That's the worst review I've ever read of any book.

"Well . . . " my husband said to me, breaking the thirty-second silence since I had begun reading. He raised his eyebrows.

"Um, I guess this next sentence sums it up nicely," I replied, clearing my throat and turning back toward the review. " 'Gives the impression of being scrawled during lunch hour for publication in a free local listings guide.' "

I looked at my husband. He looked back at me.

"That is one sucky review," he finally said.

"You're telling me," I agreed. "It's of my book. It's the *Kirkus* review of my book. And my book is about my life! My life got a bad review!"

"Listen, humor is completely subjective. If it wasn't, Carrot Top would be sleeping on the top bunk of a homeless shelter right now and selling plasma next to Andrew Dice Clay," my husband said kindly.

"Easy for you to say," I replied. "Your life isn't 'purely unappealing.' What does that even mean? It's like I'm now on a Purely Unappealing Lives list with Hitler, Pontius Pilate, Dr. Laura, and all of the other Purely Unappealing People. You know, I always thought that someone would have to see me completely naked and bending over before arriving at a conclusion like that."

My husband nodded in agreement. "It's not the best look for you," he said.

"Who hates me that much?" I wondered aloud. "I mean, someone really has to hate you to say things like that. Maybe it's Jerry. The last time he came by asking for Mountain Dew I told him that the Mountain Dew people were trying to change their image and in order to be allowed to drink it, you had to wear shoes and live in a house that wasn't towed to its present location."

"Oh, honey," my husband said sweetly. "What a beautiful world you live in! You little optimist, you! Jerry has about five brains cells left after all of the crystal meth he has sucked up his nose, and none of them resides in the literary section of his head. Jerry's brain is a ghost town. The saloon doors only swing when the wind blows. He has both the hate and anger required to write that review, I'll give you that, but I'm afraid his ability to hold a pencil was killed when he consumed an eight ball by himself in or around 1998."

"You've got a point," I agreed. "He'd kill me before he panned my book."

"You know, it doesn't matter who wrote that book review," my husband said. "It's only one person's opinion. It only matters what you think about it."

Now, deep, deep, deep in my black little rotten heart, I knew my husband was right. Sure, there were parts of the book that could have been better, funnier, tighter. Was it the best book in the world? No. But was this anonymous person going to make me believe that my book, the book that I spent almost a decade of my life trying to get published, was leaden and belonged in a local listings guide? Absolutely not, especially since there was not *one single ad* for a topless bar or phone sex in my *whole entire book*.

Besides, I was used to getting hate mail. I got it on a daily basis. This wasn't any different, I told myself, except that those people actually signed those letters. However, I had the very strong suspicion that I was going to be losing my job soon since I'd clogged the editor of the newspaper's e-mail box with a thousand letters in one night. I had already lost my weekly newspaper column and feared the death of my daily web column wasn't far behind. I had a small amount in savings and no idea what I was going to do if the book tanked, of which the chances were extraordinarily good to begin with and had now just gotten better.

Don't freak out, I told myself as I took a deep breath, you can handle it. I could find another job, embark on a new craft. I was once an optician for several years, fitting eyeglasses and contact lenses, except that while I was employed as a health care worker, I believe that I seriously maimed people. I fit one old lady named Loretta so badly with those invisible bifocals that a couple of days later she fell down a flight of stairs and got a black eye. I told her she needed to "adjust to them" because I could have lost my job for giving her a refund. The next week Loretta sideswiped a grapefruit truck and crumpled the left side of her car into a tinfoil ball. She came back and cried at the counter, to no avail. The next time I saw Loretta at the optical shop, she was armed with a surly friend who was built like a redwood. As soon as I went out to the counter, Loretta's Human Log acquaintance poked me in the chest with the arm of her BluBlocker wraparound sunglasses and then demanded Loretta's money back. Which I promptly retrieved from the cash drawer without any questions, especially when I realized the Log had only stopped poking me with her BluBlockers to raise her walking cane and hold it like a baseball bat.

Then I briefly considered joining the Peace Corps, but then again, I wasn't sure. I kept having this vision of myself sitting on some frozen mountain in a goatskin cape, the only person within a three-hundred-mile radius that had any semblance of teeth, digging through the mud with a stick to gather enough grub worms to feed an entire village for dinner.

"Oh, you should go, it sounds like a very relaxing job," my mother commented. "Just being on a foreign, tropical island and being peaceful. I hope they send you someplace good in Europe, because I want to come visit if they do. If they send you to any place like Russia, Lithuania, Poland, Croatia, Bulgaria, Finland, Latvia, Czechoslovakia, and whatever that mess Yugoslavia is today, forget it, because that's not Europe to me, you know. I mean the *real* Europe, like France, Italy, and Switzerland. Those other ones are like the runner-up Europe countries, the ones that kind of ended up there by mistake, like, you know, the boss of the United Nations said, 'Okay, Europe, if you get Sweden, you have to take the Ukraine, too, just to make it even. Otherwise, we're giving Monaco to Africa.' "

My other immediate options were to man a hot dog cart in downtown Phoenix, because I figured that was easy enough; I'd only have to work the lunch shift, and I like hot dogs. Then my bigmouth husband added his two cents after I told him my idea by laughing, "You, running a hot dog cart? You'd have to call it Exact Change Only Hot Dogs because you're so bad at math that you'd end up cheating yourself and losing everything. Besides, you're not exactly a people person."

And he was right.

I am not exactly a people person. Not exactly. You see, when I was born, God gave me an ounce of patience that was supposed to last me a lifetime, but it turns out I used all of it up during the first week.

I even have proof.

When I was six months old, my mother had my portrait taken.

The photographer apparently sensed my disgust with the whole procedure and decided to invent his own brand of hilarity by placing a small, oval plaque underneath my folded arms, droopy jowls, bored eyes, and the repugnant expression on my mean little baby face.

The little sign proclaimed boldly, I LOVE EVERYBODY.

The look on my face says, "You know, if I had even one tooth, I would sink it into your fat little arm for trying to make me look like an asshole baby. Shithead."

Now, I really need to point out that I am not indiscriminately mean; I am not mean to people whenever the mean mood strikes me. I feel that I must be provoked first, although my husband disagrees. In all honesty, I really wouldn't even identify myself as a mean person; rather, I would classify myself as a Pointer-Outer of Extraordinary Acts of Incredible Foolishness and, on Occasion, Rudeness. Some people, including my husband, would call these experiences meltdowns, but I would rather consider them Opportunities to Enlighten.

For example:

- If you are sitting behind me in a movie and you feel the need to converse as freely as if you are in your living room, I will "Shhhh!" you and then I will ask you for ten dollars. I cannot grasp the need to talk in a movie theater. If I'm going to talk to somebody, I'd rather not do it in the dark (unless I'm naked and really holding my stomach in), and if it costs me ten bucks for an hour and a half, it had better be to someone in a different state, or they'd better be telling me how hot I am. I figure if you have to talk, if you're so full of interesting and fascinating information that it is simply impossible to hold it in, THAT'S WHAT BARS ARE MADE FOR.
- If you cut me off in traffic in a *Dukes of Hazzard* move or like you've got someone in the passenger seat whose severed limb is floating in an Igloo cooler on his lap, then suddenly and inexplicably slam on your brakes for no apparent reason, I will scream, maniacally, and point my finger at you. This reaction developed

due to the fact that a moment after I bought my new car, the Insurance Institute for Highway Safety rated it as one of the suckiest automobiles ever made. If so much as a bug hits my windshield, the entire front cabin of the car will implode and it is likely that I will either be decapitated by a visor or disemboweled by the gearshift as a tragic result, now that I am driving what essentially cracks up to be a motorized casket on wheels.

- If you try to sneak two weeks' worth of groceries through the express line and think that no one will notice, I will look at your cart, look at you, and then shake my head in utter and obvious disgust. I'm done tolerating your type when all I have in my basket is a box of Monistat 7 and a pint of Chubby Hubby. I mean it. Get out of my way. Let me get my shit and go home because I have the ability to count to fifteen and I will USE IT ON YOU.
- If I happen to be looking out the window and see you allow your dog to take a shit in my yard, I will run outside with a pen and a piece of paper and query, "Hey, can I have your address? Because my dog will probably have to crap in the next hour or two, and I'm bringing her to *your* house to do it."

So I guess I am mean, I can admit that much, and because of my potential to find Opportunities to Enlighten, and the frequency with which I often stick my hands into the air, extend all my fingers, and shake my wrists in what my best friend Jamie has aptly described as the Angry Jazz Hands move, I knew at that moment that I couldn't get a job working with people; it would be disastrous. After all, a nearly blind lady was almost pummeled to a jug of Sunny Delight by a mountain of tumbling citrus because of me. I just might kill someone in my next job, and I'll be honest here, I couldn't do time. Really. No way. I couldn't share a room with four other people, let alone poop in front of them. I hate sharing a room and a bathroom with my husband, and I even have eminent domain over him. Prison would never work out: I'd get picked last for all of the gangs, I'd never get included in escape plans, it would be just like high school.

This was bad, because if my book got one nasty, horrible review, it could certainly get another. If it did, that meant that I was going to have to do something for a living besides the only thing I knew how to do.

"What am I going to do?" I cried to my husband. "This mean person hated my book, I'm losing my job, and I don't want to go to prison."

"Will you just stop with that stupid review?" my husband said, rapidly depleting the ounce that God gave him. "Who cares? I wouldn't worry about it if I were you. The amount of bad karma due that guy is probably of biblical proportions. I'm sure you're not his first victim. I wouldn't want to be the one walking next to him and wearing soccer cleats in a thunderstorm."

And just as if I had been hit by lightning myself, I had an epiphany of such revolutionary proportions that I gasped slightly.

In a millisecond, I had just hatched a brilliant, *brilliant*, magnificent plan.

If it all boiled down to bad karma, maybe the bad review was my own bad karma getting thrown back at me. Bad karma for not helping Loretta, for being impatient, for being a Pointer-Outer. And, if I could immediately embark on a life as a Nice People Person Person, maybe my next review would be good.

Really, I said to myself, how much energy could it take to be nice? A whole lot less than being angry, hostile, and frustrated nearly every time you encountered one of the Foolish, which could realistically be sixty times in one single minute if you were at the movies, the grocery store, driving someplace, or my current place of employment, I'll tell you that much. Sometimes, as a mean person, I almost had to be a *gladiator*. It took a *ton* of stamina not to melt down and just go crazy and start swinging a very sharp and pointy metaphorical sword at everybody. All you had to do to be nice was smile and nod your head. Smile and nod. And sometimes toss in a "My, what a pretty dress!" or an "Aren't you delightful?" like my seventy-six-year-old neighbor who smiles all the time despite the fact that she has a mole on her face the size of a York Peppermint Patty and two bum sons in their fifties who still live at home.

So then I practiced smiling and nodding, and *what* a piece of cake! To think I could have been doing this all along, and if I had, that bad review probably wouldn't have happened if karma had anything to do with it. After a couple of hours, I felt I was ready to start a new phase in my life, appropriately titled "I Love Everybody," and it was going to be a good day to test out my new niceness, especially as I was headed to Costco to pick up my nephew's birthday cake before his party.

As I pulled out of my driveway, I noticed my other neighbor across the street who frankly really should be living on a farm because of all the feral cats she is breeding due to the fact that she is a Feeder. Let me add to that. She should be living on a farm far, far, far away from me, because as a Feeder, she has encouraged the development of something of a free-range cat wildlife habitat in her front yard. She claims they're not her cats, but let me tell you, someone over there has to be in charge of that appalling, hideous experiment, because it's a laboratory like no other. Come stand at my window at 6 P.M. on any given night and you can see the whole show, the most extensive research project concerning crossbreeding and mammals the universe has ever hosted, *and that includes aliens*. At six is when my neighbor, the Feeder, saunters out to her front yard and pours the cheapest brand of cat food she could find that week into roughly twenty bowls scattered about her chain-link-fenced yard and slowly, you'll see the swarm begin. They come in from everywhere. They climb down from roofs, leap out of trees, crawl out from under cars, pop up out of manholes, they come. They come. And they feed, all forty to sixty of them, depending on the live-birth rate of that particular breeding season. If T. S. Eliot had lived in my house, *Cats* would have never existed; instead, there would now be a touring company of the musical *I've Got the Sack, You Bring the Rock, and We'll Meet Down by the Creek*.

I turn to the Feeder as I drive past, and really, I like her as a person. She has never said a bad word about anybody. She's truly very nice. I understand that her heart is in the right place, although her intentions should be posted on the side of a milk carton, 'cause they've done gone. I nod and I smile. She nods and smiles back. She waves.

I'm not to that level yet, but it's still nice.

Nice.

I Love Everybody.

Two miles from Costco, all is going well until a Chevy two-ton crosses two empty lanes of traffic to squeal in front of me and then reduces its speed to that of a Fred Flintstone car. It was at a barely crawling 25 miles per hour in a 45 zone that I was able to fully, and comprehensively, take in and understand the character of the motorist before me. On his bumper, for everyone to see, including his mother, his boss, his neighbors, and any womenfolk he might have swindled into dating, was a bumper sticker that read: TODAY'S WORD IS LEGS . . . LET'S SPREAD THE WORD!!

I choked on my own saliva. I don't even know what you say after seeing something like that. I really don't. Nothing except that I would be entirely remiss by not mentioning that as an additional adornment to his fine, gray-primered-on-one-side vehicle and swinging to and fro from his trailer hitch was a flesh-colored sock, into which he had apparently stuffed two racquetballs, sitting side by side, and had fashioned himself something of a scrotum. That's right, his truck had a nutsack.

His truck had a nutsack.

As I passed the Testicle Truck, I made a five-dollar bet with myself and won when I saw that its master had opted not to don a shirt that morning.

I smiled and I nodded.

"Aren't you delightful?" I said, to which he stuck his big, filthy tongue into his cheek and vigorously moved it around as he raised his eyebrows repeatedly.

I laughed and said through my smiling, clenched teeth, "Your trailer hitch has a better shot at that than you do. At least his boys have dropped."

Nice.

I Love Quite Close to Everybody.

I finally got to Costco without any more incidents—believe it or not, I didn't see any SUVs or station wagons dragging a fake uterus or fallopian tubes from the bumper—save for one small occurrence that happened as I was gunning for a prime spot in an otherwise crowded parking lot. The spot directly behind it was empty, too, so as I was a millisecond from turning into my spot, I wasn't concerned when I saw a Plymouth Valiant angle for it and begin to pull in from the opposite direction. I must confess, however, that I did feel the small rumblings of boiling blood when the Valiant did not stop once he had parked in his spot, but continued to pull on through to my spot, where he stopped, got out, winked at me, pulled up the waistband on his Sansabelt slacks, and then continued on his way as I sat watching him and he grinned, sucking on a toothpick. I smiled so hard it hurt. I nodded like a bobblehead. I turned, drove up the aisle, and took the spot he should have, and I was just as surprised as you might have been when the three-day-old and half-filled cup of hot, flat Diet Coke I was holding suddenly fell out of my hand and onto the side door of the Valiant as I was passing it. It was amazing, almost as if an Anger Angel had come up from under me and popped it right out of my grasp like a volleyball.

Maybe not so nice.

I Love Most Everybody.

At this point, I had about an hour to get the cake and drive to my sister's house before my nephew's birthday began. I had plenty of time, no sweat. I could have a nice, leisurely shopping experience. "Hi, how are you?" I said to people passing by who smiled at me, had some sort of visible ailment or challenge, or were in my way, which I figured would earn me more karma nice points, as I had a lot of catching up to do.

My first stop is always the book table. Books are to me as homemade tattoos are to an inmate. Can't get enough of them. Plus, I figured it was a good place to do some research on the niceness of other authors by looking at their photos on the jackets of their books.

What I saw shocked me. I was shocked. I was out of my league altogether. I mean, I don't know what kind of camera you have to use to capture the heavenly rays of the sun descending upon the head of a sweetly smiling, golden-locked author who is looking upward at those rays as if to say, "Yes, God, I love you. I love you, God," but it sure isn't any camera that had taken a photo of me. I mean, some of those author photos looked like prayer cards of saints that they hand out at funerals. One lady had even wrapped what looked like a very scratchy Navajo blanket around her head, Virgin Mary–style, as she gazed off into the distance over some rolling, westernlike hills through her living room window. I didn't understand that. I mean, obviously the woman had the conveniences of modern technology at hand in order to write a book, yet there she was, in her author's photo, dressed up as a Peruvian sheepherder. There weren't any sheep in the picture. I didn't even see a lamb. I guess my favorite was of a woman whose portrait was taken in profile, her head thrown back to show off her long, lean neck as she apparently laughed in a myriad complex of emotions, including elation, joy, and glee, though truthfully I thought that she somewhat resembled a seal about to catch a fish.

To sum it up, they all looked pretty damn nice, nicer than me, at least. The camera has never caught me in a spontaneous moment of exhalation so extensive it looked as if I has suddenly thrown my head back and was about to burst forth to speak in tongues, I never wandered around my home with a Native American, hand-crafted textile or even a down comforter wrapped around my head, for that matter, and honest to God, the only time I ever saw definitive rays of light streaming through my windows was when I had a two-pack-a-day Marlboro habit and the molecules of light had to slice through the fog of smoke in the house.

I flipped over the sheepherder's book to read the rave reviews, including one from *Kirkus* that made her sound as if she had, in giving birth to this book, ended hunger, child abuse, and found a cure for stretch marks. Ditto on the angelic, hazy sun gazer who looked as if she were duly prepared and expected to be, at any moment, zapped up into the sky like Captain Kirk during the first, blissful seconds of the Rapture. She was, you could tell, a definite first-string redeemer. Oh, yeah. She was going. And the seal catching the fish, she was going, too, you could just tell. Who claps their hands and tosses their heads back like that except for the devoutly religious and people whose eyes are too far apart?

I never had a chance. I didn't even qualify for stand-by Rapture status. I looked again at the sun gazer and knew I was completely out of my league. I wouldn't be at all surprised if God himself placed a 911 to the *Kirkus* reviewer on her behalf, warning that boils, humpbacks, and leprosy is what that *Kirkus* employee could expect if he even considered giving His Girl a bad review, and if he needed proof, God would add, "Look down the hall or at what's sitting in the cubicle next to you. It wasn't the asbestos, after all, chump."

I pushed my cart away from the book table feeling even more hopeless when I suddenly realized a pick-me-upper was only a freezer department away. After all, it was almost noon, and in Costco, that translates into a free hors d'oeuvres lunch, and if I was lucky, a tablespoon of Popsicle in a little paper pill cup for dessert. And nothing, almost nothing, can make me as happy as a free bit of fried food. It's kind of like happy hour, but without the drink specials and an ugly coworker trying to worm his tongue into your ear.

But as I rounded the corner I saw very much to my dismay that only one sample lady was set up and the others were still involved in their prep work, heating up their Fry Daddies and plugging in their toaster ovens. In fact, the one sample lady who was set up already had quite a crowd in front of her, because sometimes people at Costco act like the sample ladies are doling out pieces of eight or individual Viagra pills instead of one-eighth of an eggroll.

So I got in line, waiting for my free whatever it was. It was almost my turn, there were only two girls, who looked to be in their very early twenties, ahead of me, and as they chatted away it was obvious that they were together. I overheard the sample lady say to them, "Cherry, raspberry, peach, or blueberry?" and I felt my heart skip a beat. Popsicle. It's a Popsicle! I thought to myself. Maybe it's a PhillySwirl, I *love* those, different flavors of Italian ice all swirled together and they're supersugary and cold and soft but not slushy and they turn my mouth blue. This is just the shot in the arm I need.

At that precise moment, a sharp, high-pitched noise erupted in front of me that used my ear as a portal to repeatedly stab at my brain.

Brrrring! Brrrring!

"That's you," the first girl bubbled.

"No, that's you," the other girl gushed.

Brrring! Brrring! Stab! Stab!

Answer the phone, I mouthed as I tried not to wince.

"It's so totally you!" the first girl insisted.

"It is so totally *not* me!" the other girl replied.

Brrring! Brrring! Stab! Stab!

Answer the stupid phone, I said silently as I tried in vain to turn my head to avoid the auditory assault.

"Maybe it *is* me," the first girl said, staring at her friend.

"I think it *is* you!" her friend confirmed.

Brrring! Brrrring! Stab! Stab!

Answer it! Answer it! I screamed in my imagination, finally forced to cup my hands over my ears.

Then the first girl finally opened up her fishing net of a purse and began to dig through it to find the source. She grabbed it, unfolded it, and held it up to her ear.

"Hel-lo!" she demanded gleefully. "HEL-LO-OH!"

Then she sadly looked at her friend. "They hung up," she said morosely.

"Wow. Maybe it *was* me," her friend concluded.

"Ohhhhhhh," the first girl said.

"Ohhhhhhh," her friend said in sympathy. "Maybe they'll call back!"

"Cherry, raspberry, peach, or blueberry?" the sample lady said.

"Oh," the first girl said as she paused and turned toward her friend. "I don't know. I don't know. What are *you* going to get?"

"I don't know," her friend said slowly. "What are *you* going to get?"

"THE BLUEBERRY IS THE BEST," I heard myself proclaim, feeling the fire at my feet, feeling the fuse begin to light. "THE BLUEBERRY IS THE BEST, JUST GET THAT, PLEASE, YOU TWO VERY DELIGHTFUL GIRLS IN PRETTY DRESSES!"

"This is a skort, not a dress," the first girl said as she looked at me oddly.

"Really? No way! It totally looks like a cute dress!" her friend gushed.

"BLUEBERRY!" I said as I felt the uncontrollable desire to cover my head and rock back and forth. "BLUE BERRY!"

"Blueberry," the first girl said to the sample lady, still looking at me.

"Blueberry," her friend said, nearly in a whisper.

The sample lady handed them the little paper pill cup and they walked away.

I Still Love Everybody, but With a Couple More Exceptions.

"Oh my God, did you hear that?" I said to the sample lady, stepping forward and shaking my head. "Did you hear that phone? Did you *hear* that? It was like some crazy sonar signal, that sharp, *sharp* noise going into my head, God, it was like a torture device, is my ear bleeding? Is there blood there? Can you see any? I mean, where do you even get a phone like that, the Central American Secret Police Store? You could win a revolution with a phone like that. You could kill *dolphins* with that phone. That phone would *totally* kill a dolphin, they have very sensitive brains! I mean, I was trying to love those girls, *I was*, I was really trying to love them, but my God, that right there is solid proof that evolution has hit the road, baby. That's right. We're nothing but monkeys with covered nipples is all. That's all we are. Are you sure you don't see any blood?"

The sample lady smiled. "We have cherry, raspberry, peach, or blueberry. What flavor of sugar-free fruit-flavored water would you like?"

"Blu—" And then I stopped for a moment. "What? You mean to tell me I have been standing in line this whole time for sugar-free water? I waited in line for *water*? While my brain was being stabbed?

That is *not* a line-worthy sample! It is just *not*. You don't even get to chew anything! Water? Who picked *water*? I can get water for free over at the water fountain!"

"This water is free," she reminded me.

"That is not what I mean!" I said quickly. "There's—no—*line there*! I don't have to spend *time* waiting for free water! That is . . . that is what I meant!"

"You would if someone was in front of you," she remarked.

"Okay!" I said, throwing up my hands. "Fine. You win the free-water battle. It's yours. You win. Fine. I don't need any water, I came over here to chew something. When you have something to chew, when you have a *real sample*, you let me know!"

And with that, after I was sure the sample lady had been enlightened at least slightly, I walked away, and after I walked for about ten seconds, I turned around to prove my point and that's when I saw all the other sample ladies huddled with the water sample lady and she was pointing at me.

I Love Everybody, but Some People Are Simply Undeserving of the Love.

Now, with my original hour evaporating into about half of that, I needed to hurry. I got to the bakery counter, and as the baker was in the process of getting my cake, another customer, a lady with big hair, frosted in chunks, wearing a sleeveless oxford shirt with very tanned arms like tree trunks and far too much pungent perfume, came to the counter and yelled, waving her diamond-encrusted hand at the bakery lady, "Ma'am! Ma'am! I only have a question, this will only take a second!"

"I'll be right with you," the bakery lady said with a smile.

"But this will only take a second," the lady insisted. "I'm in a hurry."

"I'll be right with you," the bakery lady said again with a smile, and I waited.

"I'm sure this girl can wait, this will only take a second, and it's important," the smelly diamond lady said anyway. "That carrot cake you have over there, do you have any without walnuts? I can't eat walnuts. I am peanut sensitive."

I took a deep breath.

"The cakes on that table aren't made by this bakery, so I don't know," the bakery lady informed the frosty, stinky lady as I waited. "Those come from other vendors."

"Uh-huh," the sleeveless, big-haired lady said. "Well, I can't eat walnuts. So is there a carrot cake over there without them? My tongue swells up and I get hives. I get very itchy."

"Those aren't our cakes," the bakery lady tried to explain as I still waited. "I don't know what they have in them, we didn't make them."

"But my tongue gets big, very swollen," the pungent diamond lady said. "I have a reaction because of an allergy and it could almost kill me."

"Maybe you should try a chocolate cake, then," the bakery lady said, trying very hard to be polite, and turned around to get my nephew's cake.

"No, I can't, I'm on a diet," the big-armed peanut hater said as she turned her cart and rolled away before I could walk over and punch her.

Now, finally, with cake in hand, I sped toward the exit, through the bakery department, and toward the freezer section again and I was making good time. I was making really good time. I was flying, dodging children, precarious product displays, people running for samples. I was almost through the freezer section when my speedy progress came to a complete halt due to a lady in front of me, pushing her cart at a snail's pace, her arms crossed over the handle of the cart as she leaned on it like the very lazy person she apparently was. I tried to get around her several times, but oncoming traffic in the freezer section was at a bottleneck; the sample ladies who had been merely setting up before were now open for business, and each sample station had become its own little beehive, buzzing with activity as people stood around almost like little baby birds, their mouths open, waiting for the sample ladies to toss a nugget in.

I couldn't get around her, and she was making no effort whatsoever to pick up the pace, and I was stuck. I now had twenty minutes to get to my sister's house, and my chances of making it on time were thin at best. I tightly clutched the handle of my own cart, chanting with a clenched jaw over and over again like a mantra, "I Love Everybody, I Love Everybody, I Love Everybody, I Love Everybody," until I saw a break in cart traffic ahead and geared myself, getting ready to make a break for it. Within seconds, my chance had arrived and I took it: I jerked forward, clipping the slow, lazy lady's heel in the process, swerved over to the right as I began to pass her, walked faster and faster, gaining on her. When I was merely two steps behind her, I could no longer hold it in; I could no longer absorb it; my Bounty paper towel of patience could sop up no more. I had had enough. I had had enough of the walnut lady, the deceiver sample lady, the cell phone girls, the parking space stealer, the nutsack truck guy, and now the slow walker, and I could take no more. My load was full, it was overwhelming, and I let it out, loud and clear, so the slow walker would absolutely hear—with the visual companion of my arms raised up, fingers spread, wrists a-shakin', that's right, Angry Jazz Hands—"Here's an idea! Why don't you just drop to all fours and *crawl* through the store! That just might be slower!"

And it worked. She did indeed hear me, I saw, as my cart became parallel with hers and she turned to look at me, although she couldn't turn too much because that would have ripped the tube that was connected to her oxygen tank, which was sitting in her cart, right out of her nose. Right out of her nose. And both nostrils, too. Those tubes looked pretty short to me, as she leaned over to make sure they stayed in to keep her, well, alive.

DING! DING! DING! DING! I heard in my head, like the bell at the end of a boxing match. *DING! DING! DING! DING!* Bad review! Bad review! One order for another bad review coming right up! It's spelled N-O-T-A-R-O.

I knew I had just RSVP'ed for my own personal spot in hell, right next to the Skin Pit, across from the Pool of Sin.

Forty minutes into my nice-person experiment and I was already out of the game.

I Love Everybody as Long as I'm Alone in My House.

I ducked down a side aisle, waiting until all witnesses to my meltdown—even I couldn't consider bellowing at an old woman, whose life clock had been chiseled down to pretty much a matter of minutes, to haul her oxygen-deprived ass out of my way and giving her a flagrant, flashy display of Angry Jazz Hands as an Opportunity to Enlighten in any way—had dispersed throughout the store so that I could get out of the place without any more fingers pointing at me or a mob coming at me with a rope in tow.

I shook my head. I had failed. I had completely flunked at being nice. I was disappointed in myself—I really thought I could pull it off. I did. An hour ago I'd had so much faith in myself, I thought as I skulked down the aisle and then turned. I should be ashamed of myself. I couldn't even be nice for a whole hour.

That's when I finally looked up and found myself right back at the freezer department, square in front of the sample ladies, who were busy frying, toasting, and handing out free food.

Free food.

Free. No change needed, no change taken. No change made.

Well, why not? I said to myself, and walked over to the sample lady whose crowd was the smallest, although I couldn't help but notice a big frosted head sticking out like a sore thumb. I smiled the biggest grin I had all day when I saw the sample lady was cutting up delicious-looking cookies, and I nodded at her as I helped myself to one.

She smiled and nodded back. "These are our wonderful chocolate chip cookies," she said.

Someone from behind suddenly bumped me, and without an "Excuse me" or "Pardon me," I saw a big, tanned, diamond-encrusted arm that looked awfully familiar reach up to the sample tray and grab two cookie pieces like a goblin then suddenly retreat, almost if on cue.

I turned around and there she was, her big frosted head opening wide to pop in the cookie bits. I waited until she chewed a couple of times and I saw her swallow.

I was a bad girl.

A bad girl with nothing to lose.

"These are the most wonderful cookies I have ever eaten in my life!" I said as loudly as I could, then turned to the frosted chewing head, who nodded vigorously in agreement. It was then that I embarked on a huge Opportunity to Enlighten with a bold-faced, nutty lie. "Don't you just love chocolate chip walnut cookies? I am *crazy* about these walnuts!!"

I Tried to Love Everybody, but Sometimes, You Just Have to Hate a Little, Too.

And, with that, I turned back to the sample lady and smiled.

"That is a delightful hair net and apron you're wearing," I said. "Do you have any openings? I'd like to fill out an application."

Disneyland: A Tragedy in Four Acts

Act One: Penance, Patience, and Peanut Butter Pizza

"I don't understand," I said to my sister as I looked around us. "If this is the happiest place on earth, why are half the kids crying?"

It was true. Everywhere we went in Disneyland, whether it was waiting on line for a ride, waiting on line for food, or waiting on line to kiss Minnie Mouse, everywhere you looked, at least two out of five kids were sobbing, screaming, or hyperventilating, having either been recently smacked, recently yelled at, or recently threatened with being "sent back to the room."

I, however, was having a grand time. Somehow, either I had arrived on the perfect day or I had traveled through some sort of self-esteem time warp, but I was one of the prettiest people at Disneyland. For the first time in . . . well, *ever*, I realized that I was currently ranking pretty high on the attractiveness scale considering my competition with the rest of the adults in the park. Now, honestly, that's not saying much about me, but I will admit that every time I saw two honey-baked hams swinging out the armholes of a tank top, my self-esteem skyrocketed. A size sixteen anywhere else in the free world translated to a size four here, and I never felt so liberated. Free as a bird and, metaphorically speaking, weighing about the same as one, I found myself scarfing down a double ice-cream cone without shouting loud enough so that everyone could hear, "What do you mean this is ice cream? I ordered fat-free yogurt!"

I loved Disneyland. I LOVED IT. I had no idea I was going to have such a good time when my sister had asked me to accompany her and my nephew Nicholas to celebrate his fourth birthday, because initially, I really didn't care to go. I mean, it's Disneyland, and it has very little appeal for a childless woman in her thirties, unless her intelligence level is significantly below average. Since I'm only slightly below average, the Magic Kingdom doesn't hold as much magic for me as it is a reminder that unless I die in a freak accident relatively soon, I will die alone, withered, and childless in a rest home unless one of my nephews takes pity on me, which I doubt, since they both find me annoying, needy, weird, and clingy, though at this point, neither one can ride a bicycle with only two wheels. Despite that reminder and also because of it, I agreed to go on this trip for two reasons:

1. I try really hard to be the cool aunt, which in the world of a childless, weird, needy, clingy woman in her thirties is called Reduced-Fat Motherhood. Just enough of a taste of parenthood that you can have the experience without all of the consequences. In our family, the responsibility lies solely with me to expose Nicholas to stimuli outside of the Time Warner/AOL, McDonald's, and, yes, Disney minivan culture of suburban America. There are some good elements in that mix, certainly, but I wanted his horizons to be a bit broader than, say, *the mall*, which, you may recall, he had spent so much time at that he wanted to name his baby brother after it.

I tried my best to bring out the creative side to the kid, although some noncreative family members interpreted my goodwill as an effort to lead the boy down the wrong road, namely the one that I, myself, had taken. For his first birthday, I bought him a tambourine. For Christmas, a drum set. For his next birthday, I found a kiddie guitar. When he opened that gift, my sister sneered at me and hissed, "Why don't you just get it over with and buy the child a bong?"

"Oh God, not bongoes," my mother growled. "I have a big enough goddamn headache with those friggin' drums!"

In any case, going on this trip would give me the opportunity to have fun with my nephew, bond even closer with him, and build his trust in me so that I might wield him like a puppet and mold him into the child I absolutely knew we both wanted him to be.

2. I was also at Disneyland paying penance and trying to make up for "embarrassing and traumatizing him in front of twenty of his little friends," according to my mother, who volunteered with me a couple of months ago as a helper in Nicholas's preschool classroom for the Harvest Festival or, what they used to call in less stringently politically correct days of yore, Halloween.

Now, I will admit that perhaps I had some responsibility in the matter, but what unfolded that afternoon was in no way entirely my fault.

After the teacher introduced me as Nicholas's Aunt Laurie, she led my mother to a huge barrel full of dry pinto beans into which the kids would stick their hands and fish out little toys. After informing her of my creative nature, the teacher assigned me to the spiderweb table, where I was supposed to help little kids make a spiderweb on a piece of paper with glue and string. And that was all going fine until the first little girl I was supposed to help, Angelina-Charlize, didn't want to make a spiderweb, she just wanted to write her name. I was cool with that. That was fine. No skin off my nose. Go ahead and write your name, you know? So Angelina-Charlize wrote her name, complete with a backward r. In an attempt at helping, I told her that we should try turning the r around a bit, and that's when she *and* her little henchman, Sarah Jessica, openly mocked me.

"Aunt Gloria doesn't know how to make an r," they both chanted. "That's so sad for a grown-up."

"No, really, the r needs to face the other way," I said, trying to smile. "Would you like me to show you?"

"There's an r in my name, so I should know," Angelina-Charlize informed me as Sarah Jessica stood behind her and giggled.

"There's no r in Aunt Gloria! Aunt Gloria can't make an r, Aunt Gloria can't make an r!"

"Actually, it's Aunt Laurie, and there is an r in that, *and* I've been writing for a long time, so maybe I should know," I retorted.

"If you know, then why can't you make one?" Angelina-Charlize taunted me. "Because you can't! You can't you can't you caaaan't!"

"You know," I wanted so desperately to tell them, "you girls keep writing in your little chimpy hieroglyphics that only a mirror can read and I'll be more than happy to write you a recommendation to Klown Kollege when the time comes, because you will indeed need it."

Instead, I just smiled and said, "March to your own dyslexic drum, Angelina Calista Jennifer Aniston Lopez Drew Barrymore. I just really hope you like the circus."

That was pretty much the moment that Nicholas's teacher came over, leaned into my ear and whispered, "Maybe we should try the play area, where it's not so structured."

I had been fired from the spiderweb table. I had just totally gotten fired from the spiderweb table, *and unjustly so*, I might add! **R. R. R.** See? I know which way it goes! **R.**

But I smiled and said okay, sure, I'll move on to another area, that's fine. And as I got up, I caught the glare of my mother, who was apparently the Annie Sullivan Bean Barrel Miracle Worker, the children flocking around her as if they were at a rave and she were running the light stick concession stand, all sticking their hands in the bean barrel, pulling out little candies and toys. I shook my head. How could I compete with that? Candies and toys! I had *string and glue* and some very complicated dynamics going on at my station. I mean, when I was assigned to that table, no one happened to mention that it was a simmering hotbed of political unrest concerning the lowercase r. A wicked web indeed.

Whatever, I said to myself, I'll show them what I can do in the play area, I'll show them. Much to my relief, I saw my nephew in the play area, running what appeared to be an invisible grocery store, using his creative imagination, just like his Aunt Laurie had taught him.

"And there you go," Nicholas said to another little boy as he handed him a big fistful of air.

"Hello, sir," I said, bending over. "I would like an apple. Do you sell apples, Nicholas?"

"Yes, I do," Nicholas said, as he handed me absolutely nothing. "And my name is Mr. Booley when I'm at my store."

"Okay, Mr. Booley," I said, looking at the empty palm of my hand. "This looks like a great apple."

"It's forty dollars, please," Mr. Booley said.

I laughed. "Well, that's a little steep, don't you think?" I asked. "Safeway has apples for ninety-nine cents a pound, and I can actually see those!"

Mr. Booley was unmoved. "Well, then, maybe you should go to Safeway," he said, unflinching.

"Okay, okay, I get it," I said, putting out my hand with nothing in it. "Here's your forty dollars."

Mr. Booley looked at my hand, and I swear he scoffed.

"My store only takes credit cards," he informed me.

"Did *he* give you a credit card?" I asked, pointing to the customer before me.

"He's *a little boy*, Aunt Gloria," Mr. Booley reminded me. "He doesn't have credit cards. Are any of your credit cards still good?"

"I think maybe you've been talking to Grandma about my credit status, but let me assure you that it is almost cleared up now," I told him. "Maybe I *will* go to Safeway! And you *know* my name is Aunt Laurie!"

"GRANDMA!" Mr. Booley yelled to my mother, who was perched over the bean barrel, getting a hug from the backward r girl. "Aunt Gloria shoplifted! She shoplifted my apple!"

"I did not! And his prices are highway robbery!" I exclaimed, trying to defend myself. "Would you pay forty bucks for an apple? Plus twenty-one percent interest? *Would you?*"

"Give the apple back, and don't buy anything else from Mr. Booley's store, do you understand?" my mother said from behind clenched teeth as the whole class turned to stare at me.

"*There is no apple!*" I tried to explain, showing everyone my empty, appleless hands. "You can't steal something that doesn't exist! There is *no apple!*"

"I saw her take a banana, too," Mr. Booley's other customer squealed.

"Maybe you'd like to cut out some paper bats over there in the corner," Nicholas's teacher came to me and said. "It's a much quieter task."

So that was why I was at Disneyland. I thought it would make up for the alleged, imaginary fruit thievery incident, especially if I maxed out the one relatively good credit card I had left at the Disney Store before the fifteenth of the month.

Now, I quickly learned that this trip wasn't as much a vacation as it was an extreme sporting event. Earlier that morning at the "Character Breakfast" in Goofy's Kitchen ($35 to have the Mad Hatter hop around your table like a flea as you're trying to eat your Mickey Mouse waffles and peanut butter and jelly breakfast pizza), I asked Nick what he had planned for his big day at Disneyland.

"Well, I would like to meet Mickey Mouse," he said as I smiled at his humble expectations. "And then I'd like to ride all roller coasters, some of them twice, go to Tom Sawyer Island, climb Tarzan's Treehouse, get in the Safari Boat, see all the movies, hug all of the characters, and then eat food from room service."

"Hey, how are those waffles?" Mad Hatter asked as he hopped back to our table. "They should make Mad Hatter waffles! Mad Hatter waffles! Waffles with a big hat! Those are the kind of waffles I'd eat!"

"You know, we could have grabbed a bagel outside for two bucks, but then the delight of having a neurotic midget dressed as Oscar Wilde buzz around us like a palmetto roach as I'm getting ready to gorge on my breakfast lasagna would have been lost forever," I told my sister.

Suddenly, my nephew squealed, "Goofy! Goofy!! Over here, Goofy, over here! It's my birthday!"

I turned around, and there he was; that giant dog thing or walrus or whatever he is suddenly appeared, pulling the little children toward him like safety pins to a magnet.

"Oh, Goofy, please come here! Please! It's my birthday!" my nephew cried, waving his arm frantically.

"It's my un-birthday! Come to *my* tea party!" the Mad Hatter warbled to no one.

Suddenly, Goofy noticed Nick and made a beeline for us, as Nicholas jumped out of his seat and gave Goofy a big hug.

"Oh, sure," the Mad Hatter spouted. "Goofy's hot. Everyone loves Goofy. No one loves the Mad Hatter. They all want Goofy!"

"I love Goofy!" my nephew said, going in for another hug as Goofy patted his head.

"Goofy thinks he's all that, but he's *not*," the Mad Hatter continued. "You'll hug Goofy but you won't hug me. But let me tell you something, Goofy is not as hot as he thinks he is. Are you, Goofy? Are you?"

And then, as both my sister and I turned to look at Goofy and Nicholas, we both saw that Goofy's middle finger—and I mean there was no mistaking it, since he only has three of them—was vividly scratching his nose, the finger on either side folded under.

"I think somebody slipped some serious acid into my Mickey Mouse waffles," I whispered to my sister, who had the very good sense to press the "record" button on her video camera as soon as the Mad Hatter started to lose his shit. "Or did I not just see Goofy flipping off the Mad Hatter?"

"Uh-huh," she replied, her mouth open, aghast.

"That is the coolest thing I've ever seen, with or without the benefit of pharmaceuticals," I said, completely amazed. "I'd totally give them both fifty bucks to fight."

Before I had a chance to access an ATM for the loot, the Mad Hatter was busy annoying someone else and Goofy had moved to a table where an unattended toddler was trying to feed him a Danish through his mesh mouth.

Act Two: The Lair of the Pooh

Our first stop at Disneyland, as dictated by the birthday boy, was to find Winnie-the-Pooh, which we did in his little designated hundred-foot wood. As we stood in line to wait our turn, something suddenly struck me.

"I just realized that most of these characters are highly indecent," I said as I looked around. "If Donald Duck can throw on a shirt, why can't he put on pants? Look at Winnie-the-Pooh over there. He's totally exposed from the waist down. If anyone else approached a kid dressed like that, they'd be doing three to five!"

My sister pretended to ignore me.

"It's an astute observation," I continued, apparently to no one in particular. "Personally, I think it's about time somebody said something. I mean, if you can't even say the word 'Halloween' in a classroom, somebody ought to tell Winnie that he needs to cover up his . . . *stuff*, even if he is all smooth right there. It's the implication, is what it is."

Soon, Nicholas was in front of the line, and when it was his turn to cavort with the half-naked characters, my sister flashed me a look that told me not to ruin it for my nephew.

Frankly, however, this wasn't the first time my family had encountered something of a problem with the Winnie-the-Pooh crew. Not the first time at all. As soon as my sister gave birth to Nicholas, it gave her a valid reason to go to Disneyland, a place that she truly loves, every three months without getting odd looks and comments from the rest of us. Therefore, it wasn't surprising at all when she bundled up her then eight-month-old baby and took him to the Magic Kingdom. With my parents in tow.

They packed up the minivan and hauled the car seat, a bouncy chair, several strollers, a playpen, enough toys to open a day-care center, and headed to California for a five-hour drive. My mother, who can get carsick simply by touching the door handle of the backseat, was really in no mood for shenanigans once they reached Disneyland and found Winnie-the-Pooh's lair. It was never really clear whose idea it was that all five of them be in the group photo with Pooh and his posse, and after what happened, it's obvious why.

Eeyore did a nasty to my mom.

It's true, my mother swears up and down, that the purple, clinically depressed four-legged creature handled her. She stoutly contends to this day that as the photo was about to be taken with Piglet and Tigger, Eeyore reached over to feign putting his arm around her and instead served himself a hungry man's helping of rump cheek with his aubergine hand, or paw, or hoof, or whatever.

Typically, my mother would have reached up with one of her sculptured nails and popped his big googly eyeball right off his big felt head, but nausea had the best and feistiest of her, and the only violence she could summon up against Eeyore was a disgusted look. When I asked her what she said, she replied with, "Well, what the hell do you think I said? I said, 'You know, you're weird in the videos I've seen, and I don't care how sad you are because nothing goes your way, you're a sicko! A sicko! You know that? That's why things don't ever work out for you, you friggin' sick donkey!' "

I knew enough to stay away from the big purple menace during this encounter, that's for sure, I didn't care how harmless and despondent the predator seemed. I understood now how Eeyore could have thought my mom was pretty hot compared with what he saw on a daily basis, and frankly, if he went for my mom's caboose, I was in big trouble, considering how absolutely delightful I looked in comparison to other park attendees. The last way I wanted to spend my day at Disneyland was screaming for security to come and get a huge-ass horny donkey off me after he knocked me flat to the ground, his pinned-on tail swishing wildly in anticipation.

For Mr. Winnie-the-Pooh, however, I had other plans. While he stood there, watching my nephew getting hugged by Tigger, I felt I had no choice but to say something; after all, this probably was going to be my one and only opportunity to confront him about his quite liberal apparel policy.

"You know," I said point-blank to him, "would it kill you to put on some pants? I mean, really now. The kid's like thirty inches tall, which is *guess where* on you? Have a little respect, you know what I'm saying?"

Winnie just shrugged and then patted me on the shoulder.

"What does *that* mean?" I replied as Winnie blatantly walked away from me. "You know, if I showed up to work dressed in your outfit, they'd send me for an 'evaluation,' then I'd get sued for sexual harassment, plus, no one would ever eat lunch with me again. Maybe in the porno world it's a bit different, but *out there*, you'd eat every honey pot alone, mister!"

It was at that moment that Winnie tapped my nephew on the shoulder and invited the thirty-inch kid to come in for an out-and-out bear hug, and then motioned my sister to get in on the deal, too, which she vigorously joined, like Winnie-the-Pooh was Brad Pitt. I stood there for a long time watching, an outsider, an outcast.

Then Winnie looked up from the love fest and waved at me, made my nephew wave, and then made my sister wave. I don't care, I thought to myself. I don't. Go ahead and wave. Exclude me. I'm the only one brave enough to say what we are all thinking, or at least, what perhaps only a few but *very observant* people are thinking, or maybe if even I am alone in my observations, marching around in a theme park like it is some half-nude nudist colony is still not very polite, even if you are supposed to be a cartoon character.

"Winnie thought you were very funny," my nephew said as we got to Toon Town. "And I think you're silly, Aunt Laurie."

"Mmmm-hmmmm, yes, I know, but when you're older, they call it 'manic depression,' " I said, nodding as I caught the glare of my sister, which told me not to ruin *this* experience for the boy, too.

Act Three: "—All Wet, She's Cry—"

"I love Gadget's Go Coaster!" my nephew said to me as we came closer to the boarding platform. "You'll ride the ride, too, won't you, Aunt Laurie?"

"Of course," I said, remembering my sister's look and trying my best not to be a Mr. Booley and the Forty Dollar Apple Spoilsport. "It's your birthday, how could I not?"

My sister and nephew climbed into the last seat of the last car, which was shaped like a round, bulbous, hollowed-out acorn, and only sported a seat big enough for two. I hopped into the seat in front of them, and my nephew squealed with glee as the train took off. The whole ride, which was a basic, no-frills kiddie roller coaster sporting props of oversize combs, big gears made from huge bottle caps, wooden blocks, and a couple rather large stationary frogs, lasted no more than a minute, so when the train pulled to the boarding platform at the end, Nicholas said he wanted to go again.

Off we went on the Go Coaster, making another round, and as we pulled up to the platform this time, Nicholas said he wanted to go yet again as the other five people on the ride got off, leaving the whole train empty except for the three of us.

I turned around to tell Nicholas how cool it was that we got to go on the next Go Coaster trip alone, but the seat behind me was empty. They were gone. Vanished.

Puzzled, I looked around, thinking, "Oh, I get it, I get it. This is my punishment for setting Winnie-the-Pooh straight. I get ditched. Aunt Laurie gets blown off, and now I get to look stupid and wander around Toon Town trying to find my family while they spy and laugh at me from behind Goofy's Bounce House. Very nice. *Very nice*," when suddenly, I saw the two of them running along the boarding platform and then quickly jumping into the very first seat of the very first acorn four cars ahead of me.

Before I could even say anything, much less move up near them, the train took off and there I was, alone at the back of the train, riding this kiddie roller coaster essentially all by myself. My nephew was shrieking and having a delightful time far, far, *far* ahead of me, and I was trying to concentrate on his fun when we turned a bend in the ride, and then suddenly out of nowhere, something hard and fast struck me in the side of the head.

I grabbed my skull, which was now wet with a liquid I was really hoping was not a body fluid, like blood, and that's when I saw it. That's when I saw what I had just passed, which was the seemingly placid, peaceful, unaggressive frog statue until it decided to spit at you with a fire hose of water that was conveniently hidden from view. I was still trying to wipe the water from my face when we pulled into the boarding station next to an empty platform.

"Wanna go again?" the conductor yelled to Nicholas, who promptly responded with a joyous round of yesses, and the conductor took off for our next round without even stopping.

This time, I knew where that goddamn frog was and prepared myself to be spat upon, and when I finally breathed a sigh of relief that I had not been attacked again, we were back in the station with a still-empty platform.

"AGAIN?" the conductor shouted happily, not even slowing down as we headed for another trip.

"Hey!" I shouted from the last acorn, which was apparently a sound vacuum, as we roared ahead. "You guys, I'm done with this ride! Aunt Laurie is done!"

PPPLLLLTTT!! went the frog as I passed him again, hard and fast like the first time and just as wet.

"AGAIN?" the conductor screeched as we rounded the corner and approached another empty platform.

And there I was, there I was, a wet, childless woman in her thirties, riding solo in the very last mammoth acorn on a kiddie ride, trying to wipe water out of her eyes, one side of her head dripping with frog spit, as she went around and around and around the Go Coaster, people in Toon Town walking by and mumbling audibly as I passed *again* and *again* and *again*;

"—poor little—"

"—all alone—"

"—bet she's backward—"

"—not a friend in the—"

"—all wet, she's cry—"

"—should call CPS—"

"—tard—"

Now, honestly, it's not the first time I've been mistaken for a person who's wiring has shorted out a bit, but it stings just the same every time, every time.

Finally, THANK GOD, someone was on the platform when we came around the last time, much to the chagrin of the popular ride people in the very first row, who got out of their seat and walked away like I wasn't even there, *way behind them* in the last lonely acorn.

"HEY!!" I shouted after my sister, who was busy laughing with my nephew as they raced to another ride. "Hey! Wait, you guys! Wait for me! *Please!*"

"What happened to you?" she said when she saw me and eventually stopped. "You look awful! Well, at least it's not as bad as what I just heard. I heard there was a little mentally challenged girl on some ride around here who wouldn't stop crying. Cried till she was sopping wet. Isn't that sad?"

"That's sad," my nephew seconded.

"The frog on your ride hocked on me, you know, and wrecked my pretty supermodel hair," I complained. "And I think it also left a hematoma where the spray hit me in the head. It's all soft and squishy in that spot now."

Act Four: Raising the Stupid Death Bar

"Gadget's Go Coaster made me ready for Splash Mountain," Nicholas asserted. "Can we go, Mommy?"

"Oh, *come on*, dude!" I whined as I stomped my foot. "I already look like a sponge! Splash Mountain? Let's go back to the hotel and eat room service stuff, okay? It's on me. Eighteen-dollar grilled cheese sandwiches for everybody!"

Nicholas shook his head. "Splash Mountain," he demanded.

"Hmmm, does Splash Mountain have a backward *r* in it?" my sister said, looking me dead in the eye and rubbing her chin for emphasis. "Does it? I can't remember, Aunt Gloria, does it?"

"Okay, fine," I surrendered. "I am here to pay for my sins. I've already been baptized at Disneyland, I just don't want to drown."

"Just don't sit in the first seat," my sister said. "Those people are the only ones who get wet."

I really had no choice. I nodded, surrendered, and walked with my sister and my nephew into the entrance of Splash Mountain.

"Now, remember, don't do something stupid and get out of your seats on this ride," the man in front of us told his two nearly teenage sons. "A guy died on this ride not too long ago when he tried to do that."

A look of panic washed over my sister's face. "Excuse me, what?" my sister said as she tapped the man's shoulder. "Someone died on this ride?"

"One more round at Gadget's Go Coaster and I'd be dead," I offered to no one. "That ride tried to lobotomize me."

"Sure did, but at the one in Disney World." The man sighed. "Got gored by a big log coming the other way, full of people. I saw it on CNN. No way you coulda stopped that thing, logs don't have brakes." I was stunned, but also felt a tremendous sense of relief. The Stupid Death Bar had now been raised to such proportions that even I couldn't reach it in my final moments, even if they rolled out the way I had anticipated them to. I always imagined I would die one of two ways: taunting a wild animal at the zoo until the lion, tiger, or Kodiak bear bursts through their defective cage and mauls me, peeling the skin off my head like a grape; or that I am killed by my own car when it suddenly lurches forward as I try to open the back gate so I can park and I become trapped between the two. In this scenario, however, I do not die immediately; it takes an extended period of time, such as overnight, for me to finally succumb, during which I call my husband's name over and over in a cry for help. However, he at the same time finds it remarkable that an unseen character on a *Law & Order* marathon has the same name as he does, although the mysterious phantom is never seen in the show.

Before I knew it, I was hustled into a log, sitting in the second seat behind one of the almost teenage sons of the guy ahead of us in line.

He looked at the wet side of my head and gave me a pained smile.

"I know you were hoping to be straddled by a skinny blonde cheerleader with perfect skin and a Crest Nighttime Whitening Strips smile," I let him know. "But an hour ago, I was the hottest chick in this park."

He grimaced visibly and moved forward on the log before we lurched and then took off.

I wonder if I am in the killer log? I asked myself as we climbed the first incline and I heard my nephew squeal with anticipation directly behind me. What's that there? Is that blood? Why would you even want to get out here? I thought, looking around. It's not like there's a $12 funnel cake stand or a Cinnabon up here somewhere. Not even a gift shop. Nowhere to buy mouse ears, I kept thinking as we reached the top, paused for a moment, and then dropped furiously downward, and that's when I gasped.

Because that's when it hit me: When you're about to dive into a pool of water from four stories up going roughly 30 to 40 miles per hour and you're wearing a white T-shirt with a white nylon bra underneath it, there's a very good reason to try to get the hell out of that car.

A very good reason.

"I told you not to sit in the front of that log," my sister insisted as we walked out of Splash Mountain. "I told you if you sat in the front of the log, this would happen."

"I wasn't sitting in the *front*," I snapped. "I was in the second seat."

"The only thing protecting you from that wave was a scrawny twelve-year-old boy who provided about as much of a shield as a chicken breast," my sister said. "Would you please step back? You are dripping all over me."

"Well, I'm glad that I was of service to you," I shot back. "Thanks to my effectiveness as a shield, the both of you are as dry as dirt."

"Did you know that wet, you have Liza Minelli's hair?" my sister asked. "And now your makeup looks like hers, too."

"Why are your arms crossed?" my nephew said. "Are you mad?"

"I'm not sure if 'mad' is the word, Nicholas," I answered. "I'm just trying to keep our little trip here at a G rating. If I uncross my arms, either I'd get taken away by or I'd pop up in the latest version of *Totally Ugly Girls Gone Wild*."

"Oh, you look fine," my sister tried to reassure me. "It's not that bad!"

"Oh yeah?" I said, lifting up one of my elbows.

"Whoa," my sister remarked. "Last time I saw one of those roaming around in the open it was frolicking with Tommy Lee on a boat. But really, the parts of you that aren't actively pornographic look . . . okay."

"Really?" I asked, clinging to one last shred of hope. "I started out so great this morning, and now I look like a used Bounty paper towel."

"No," my sister said as she shook her head. "If you were wearing that, you wouldn't look so completely topless."

"Let's go to Tom Sawyer Island!" Nicholas quipped.

"Fine with Aunt Laurie," I said. "She needs to find some sun before she gets nominated for adult entertainer of the year."

Over on the island, my nephew and my sister ran through caves and climbed up forts like chimps with a bunch of other kids, and I tried my best to keep up, but I lost them in the labyrinth of Injun Joe's Cave, being that I couldn't move very freely without exposing myself to a random child. In favor of keeping my balance and remaining upright, I decided to try and backtrack my way out and then find a nice sunny spot where I could dry out and enjoy the benefits of opaque clothing again. Finally, I saw the opening of the cave and headed toward it, and as I entered daylight, I suddenly saw the tumble of sky, the sun, glimpses of blurry faces, and finally, a big patch of brown all tossed in front of me like a salad.

When I looked up, I heard a chorus of tiny giggles and saw a bunch of rotten kids above me on the mountain, peering over and cackling like Children of the Corn. I had totally eaten it on Tom Sawyer Island, which wasn't surprising since my arms were entirely useless. As I got up from my full-body dirt sprawl, grasping at the base of the mountain, I tried to act cool, like it was no big deal, while the kids still chortled.

I looked down at myself, and I saw three mud circles; one formed perfectly over each already wet boob, then a particularly large one that covered the spot where my big, fat belly is—and the skin on my palms had been scraped away.

Well, I thought, at least I'm not naked anymore. I am emotionally destroyed and physically devastated, but I am no longer flashing.

When my sister finally came around the corner with my nephew in tow, I had only one thing to say to them.

"Hi," I said coolly as they both stared at the big brown mounds. "I HATE DISNEYLAND."

God's Car Wash

I saw it as I came around the front of my car, a streak of glistening silver, long, stretched, and shiny across the hood.

I looked at it curiously, tilting my head the way a dog does when he doesn't understand you or the way my husband does when I ask him to do his own laundry.

At first, I thought that someone had hocked a huge one onto the car, but the stain was far too large for that. I came around to the driver's side and saw that the side mirror, door, and trunk had also been savaged, and as I stepped in closer to get a better look at the shiny mess, I heard it distinctly.

CRUNCH.

An eggshell.

I had been egged. An entire generation of unborn chicks had been lobbed through the air to strike and splatter all over my innocent Honda. As I scratched away hardened egg whites with my fingernail below the window, I moaned.

Now I was gonna have to wash it, something I hadn't done since I bought the car two years ago, and with good reason. What kind of idiot criminal would steal a filthy car when there's plenty of clean ones to be had? I figured no one was going to steal a car with so much nicotine on the windows that you couldn't see out in spots. No one was going to steal a car in which you had to move heavy objects like large panes of glass, my great-grandfather's meat grinder, and an old computer in order to sit down. No one was going to steal a car that would make them dirty just by riding in it. Besides, I knew that if you waited long enough, God always washed it for you.

I looked at my car, dipped in so much egg that it was ready to be breaded like a cutlet. What did this mean? I thought. Obviously, someone hates me. Eggs? What is that supposed to say? "Sadly, I am unable to appropriately express my anger, so I have no other alternative than to throw an animal product at your mode of transportation"? But pelting a breakfast food at my car? Why couldn't they just Corn Pop or Sugar Smack me?

And what's next? If eggs are the first level of vengeance, I wondered, then what? If I make the vandals even angrier—maybe by pointing out an obvious though kindly overlooked physical flaw—do I get a rasher of bacon? If I start dating their ex-spouse, what fate lies in store for me then? Will I come out of the house one day and find, to my horror, that the Honda has been Rooty Tooty Fresh 'N Fruitied, with the tires slashed and filled with whipped cream?

And who are these vandals? Who could hate me enough to throw a delicate ovum onto the hood of my car and watch it rupture?

Quickly, I assembled a list of possible and cowardly suspects.

SUSPECT #1: The President of My Neighborhood Association. MOTIVE: The fact that I tried to egg his house for reporting me to the City of Phoenix for having a messy yard, but realized it was both immature and wrong when I arrived and he was standing outside with a video camera in his hand. ULTERIOR MOTIVE: He had a sudden epiphany that when he drove by on Saturday and I extended a cordial greeting, at which he smiled and waved, I was really saying, "I hate you, stupid tattletale! Don't you wave at me, Stupid Tattletale Man!! I'm going to tattle on YOU! ON YOU!! For being DUMB, you dummy!!" (I'm not very good at on-the-spot insults.)

SUSPECT #2: Jerry, the Homeless Tree Trimmer. MOTIVE: The complete and utter rejection he experienced on the porch of my house at 11 P.M. on a Sunday night while demanding that I give him money. The main reason I don't think it's him is because my neighbor

Robyn finally called the cops on him that same Sunday night, after he stood on her porch and repeatedly said to her, "Do you recognize me? I got my hair cut. But it's me, it's really me. Here, pretend my fingers are bangs," and we're pretty sure he now sleeps in a bunk bed and shares a metal potty with four other guys.

Suspect #3: The Lady at the Movies Who Cut in Front of Me in the Popcorn Line. Motive: When the Popcorn Guy said, "I can help the next person," and it was really *my* turn but Suspect #3 stepped up to the counter, I walked up next to her and said loudly, "Cheater, Cheater, Panty-Eater!" She then gave me a dirty look and said, "Humph!" to which I put my hands on my hips and said "Humph!" much louder.

Suspect #4: The nearly dead lady breathing out of an oxygen tank at Costco whose heel I clipped with my shopping cart on the day I was supposed to be loving everybody, but she was moving way too slow and something had to be done. Motive: I almost killed her when as I passed her, I flashed a Bob Fosse–caliber Angry Jazz Hands move that shocked her so completely it came close to ripping her oxygen tube out of her nose.

When my husband came home that night, I showed him the list and told him about my car getting egged.

"Oh yeah?" he replied. "Well, I wouldn't worry about it. You've got the equivalent of all of Mount St. Helen's ash on the hood alone, that should protect it. Your little dirt cocoon should be just fine."

"I told you," I replied. "God washes my car when He thinks it's time!"

"Laurie," my husband said, "your car is so messy people have asked me if you're breeding chickens in the backseat and are then making sausage with that grinder. Maybe someone just felt sorry for your car and they're forcing you to wash it, like an intervention."

"You know I keep it messy for a reason. I keep it messy so it won't stray, kinda the same way I kept shoving chicken-fried steaks down your throat," I said, stomping around the house, collecting a bucket, sponge, and dog shampoo, since we were out of soap. "God knows better, but fine!"

With a spoon and a paper towel, I scraped the egg, which had now hardened to the consistency of polyurethane, off the afflicted areas. Then I squirted the dog shampoo on the car, worked it up into a lather, and as I took the hose to it, most of my neighbors came out to watch.

I was drying off the last part of the bumper when I heard something hit the hood. I heard another thud, and another one. I ran to the front of the car, and that's when I saw them. Three big wet streaks across the section I had just scraped.

I looked up, held out my hand, and barely got to the front porch before God's Car Wash opened for business.

Flight of the Bumblebee

As soon as I saw the pilot heading toward the main door of the school, dressed in his clean, crisp blue uniform and carrying a globe, I knew I was in a big pot of trouble.

Here I was, a guest speaker at a middle school for Career Day, and I hadn't brought one single prop.

Not one. I hadn't even pulled into the parking lot and already I was a miserable failure.

When I had been asked months ago to be a guest speaker at Career Day and attend a luncheon afterward at a local middle school, I was thrilled beyond belief. Me! Could anyone believe it? Someone out there thought I had a *career*!

I, obviously, knew better. Although my business card still said I was a columnist, in my messy little office at the newspaper, far, far away from the rest of my department, I definitely knew better. After losing my weekly newspaper column, it didn't take a genius to figure out that the survival of my daily web column was hanging on by a thread. This was confirmed one day on the homepage when my column sig—a little caricature that looked far more like a Muppet than it did me—and link to my column was no longer there, much to my surprise. I had been booted. Bumped. Eighty-sixed.

Well, you might say to yourself, there are plenty of reasons why a columnist's sig would be replaced, especially on the homepage of a newspaper's website, which changes continuously—breaking news, a latest development in a big story, or an anticipated verdict may have just been handed down. Plenty of reasons. And I would agree. Except that my tiny little Muppet head was gone, and in its place was the head of a dog.

It was the head of Mr. Winkle.

Mr. Winkle, a real dog that looks like a stuffed toy, who does nothing but pant excessively and get dressed up in outfits to take pictures with fake butterflies and rainbows and has several books, calendars, and *Today* show appearances to his name, was in my spot.

Now, some people—including the editor who put Mr. Winkle on the homepage—might reason, "Well, big deal, it's just a dog, so he took your spot for one day, it's not all that bad, you should grow up," but then I would be forced to point out that there was a pretty good chance that none of those people had ever come to work and found a two-pound dog, panting like an asthmatic and dressed up like an asshole bumblebee sitting in their spot.

Pretty good chance of that.

Despite being fired from seven jobs, despite having a gun pointed at me during one job interview, despite learning that I got a pink slip at another publication to make room for a guy who worked for *Hot Rod* magazine, I had no other choice but to make a poster officially declaring this as the lowest point in my career, and I hung it on the window of my office, facing out.

Even though my column sig returned to the homepage the next day, Mr. Winkle was a sign. I realized that my "career" at the newspaper was nothing more than a time card and inclusion in group health coverage with a lousy copay, and any other aspirations I had at my current place of employment were simply a case of misplaced hope that I needed to drown like a sack full of ugly.

And now, not only did I have a serious dent in my career on Career Day, but I had no props to boot.

"Stupid pilot," I said to myself as I tried to find a parking space. "Getting all dressed up and bringing a globe! Snotty. That is so snotty! How can anyone else compare to that? He brought the *goddamned world*. He brought the *goddamned world* as a prop."

I swung around the crowded lot, looking everywhere for a space to park in, and I zoomed toward what looked like the last empty spot. And, when I discovered that although roughly 80 percent of the space was indeed empty, the remaining 20 percent was being currently occupied by the two sets of rear tires belonging to a brightly and professionally painted massive race car trailer. A race car trailer that hauls race cars. RACE CARS.

You have *got* to be kidding me! I cried mournfully to myself as I hit the steering wheel and yelled at the trailer. And pointed at it. Not only do you need about sixteen thousand parking spaces to park your crap, but you brought a race car, too! God! Who else is here to show off and show everyone what a loser Career Day speaker I am? Maybe Jesus is here, do you think they invited Jesus? I'll probably see him in about a minute, standing in between the race car driver and the pilot, holding a loaf of bread, a fish, and a jug of water. "Hello, I am the son of God, your Lord, your Savior. Is anyone hungry? Really, don't be shy. I fed a whole Phish concert with half this much last week."

Finally, after abandoning the search for a space, I parked my car on the street and headed into the school, right behind the police officer accompanied by his bomb-sniffing dog and what I hoped was a chiropractor with a skeleton in tow and not a serial killer with a trophy. I stood in line behind them at the office to find out where I was supposed to be, as the dog sniffed the skeleton and the serial killer thought he was being very funny by making the bony hand pet the dog's head.

When it was my turn to get an assignment, I stepped toward the receptionist and gave her my name.

She looked above the rims of her glasses and eyed me suspiciously. "And you are here for . . . ?" she asked.

"Career Day," I said, shrugging. "Just like the guy with the dog and the guy with his victim."

"Oh," the receptionist replied, seeming a little taken aback. "I'm sorry, I didn't realize. You just don't have any . . . accessories. Just one moment."

It was at this specific point that I really wished I had paid closer attention in high school chemistry class so that I may have realized my true occupational dream of inventing a pill that would get rid of crappy songs running through your head within twenty seconds of taking it. Imagine the hero I'd be *then.*

Ain't nothin gonna break my stride
Nobody's gonna slow me down, oh no

Zap. Thank you, Matthew Wilder, you heinous madman who created a supersize nugget of auditory torture and then threw it out into the world! With my pill, you're beautifully smothered by obscurity once again.

I want my
baby-back baby-back baby-back baby-back ribs

Kaboom. No thanks, Chili's; with my pill, you can stick your ribs up your baby-back ass, because your jingle is a crime against humanity, and I will bleed for you no more.

Who let the dogs out
Who! who! who! who—

Splat. Nope, not this time, with my pill, those dogs aren't getting stuck in the loop of my skull. On the contrary! Round up those puppies and break out the sodium Pentothal, because those dogs aren't going out, they're going down.

But no. I wanted to be a writer—well, not really, I wanted to be an artist, but my dad simply said, "Like hell if I'm going to pay for college tuition to art school so you can spend four years smoking and making pots."

And now here I was, hands empty, with nothing. If I had invented that pill, I could have come armed with a bunch of K-Tel CDs and vials of pharmaceuticals. Why, the classrooms would fight over me!

Instead, I had nothing to offer these children. Honestly, what were the tools of my trade? Did I even have any? How could I actually tell them that in order to do my job, the most valuable instrument that I possessed were my fingers, most or all of which have been up my nose and in other various unsavory places? I mean, *think* about that. Does a plumber stick a wrench up his nose? Certainly not if it was included in a matching Craftsman set. Does a carpenter pop a zit with his hammer? Not unless it's life-threatening.

All I could really do was wave my ten little filthy, repugnant, and wanton Indians at the crowd of honest, innocent faces and request that they wash their own hands with alcohol after touching mine, especially after I really gave it some thought.

What was I thinking when I accepted this invitation? Why had I even come? What was I going to say? Now, I'd really like to report that when the door to the classroom opened and I saw the sea of wide-eyed, impressionable faces on the laddies and lasses before me that I became the Sir-ess With Love whose tongue immediately untangled and bestowed an incredible tale of honor, morality, and wisdom upon thirty-odd sets of hungry ears gathered at my knee, sitting cross-legged in a semicircle, and afterward, I played a jaunty tune on my flute that the able-bodied children danced to as if we were in medieval times and the less fortunate enthusiastically accompanied me on tambourine, but that did not happen.

That did not happen at all.

Instead, I was faced with thirty twelve-year-olds who were waiting for me to say something. And all I could think of was, This is the hand I type and wipe with.

So I just stood there.

The teacher, a cool, young hip chick named Ms. Ward, tried to save my drowning hide by diverting her pupils' attention.

"Well, Miss Notaro, did you bring any of your columns with you that we could pass around?" Ms. Ward asked me in her teacher voice.

"No," I whispered back to her. "They're only in seventh grade. I didn't want to get you fired!"

"Oh," Ms. Ward replied as she smiled and wrung her hands. "Oh! Oh! I know! You write—I'm sorry, excuse me—Kevin! KEVIN! Kevin, what is that you're squirting all over your face? What is that? Where did you get it? That's not glue that you're going to peel off later and eat, is it?"

Kevin, who I had noticed was busy rubbing something vigorously into his complexion, looked suddenly sheepish and ashamed. "It's pimple medicine," he said quietly. "The lady doing the facials was giving out samples."

"She gave me a little lipstick and some body glitter," a girl with braces piped up from the back row.

"Mrs. Hall's class has a veterinarian," a tiny blonde girl raised her hand and offered. "And he brought puppies."

"Mr. Van Dyke's class has a baker and they're eating cupcakes, I heard!" a rather portly child said.

"As I was going to say, class, Miss Notaro writes a column for her newspaper's website," Ms. Ward said. "Let's gather around the computer station and have a look!"

Before I could say anything, before I could protest loudly enough, before I even had a chance to pull out my flute and blow the first notes to "Greensleeves," the newspaper's website was up on a computer and the kiddies gathered around it—astonishingly pointing, laughing, and gasping in bewilderment and awe.

"Wow, look at that," I heard the tiny blonde girl say. "That's so cool!"

Honestly, I couldn't help but smile to myself in a little, teeny-weeny moment of pride. Maybe it was going to be all right. Maybe I wasn't such a Career Day loser after all, maybe I did have something to share with the little tots. As I looked toward the computer screen, then put my hand on the blonde girl's shoulder, I anticipated an invigorating round of question and answer, in which my smallish, delightful apprentices would put down their acne cream, stop dreaming of puppies licking their faces while they ate cupcakes, and inquire one after another about just how in the world they, themselves, could become Laurie Notaro, web and newspaper columnist. Me. Looking forward to that moment, I smiled a little broader, and felt myself blush.

The tiny little blonde girl looked up at me and then at my hand, which I removed quickly.

"Why is his tongue sticking out like that?" she asked.

"I'm sorry?" I said.

"Is that real or not?" the chunky boy beside her asked. "It just looks like a stuffed animal to me."

"Why is it all dressed up like a bee?" another child inquired.

"I don't see your column up here," Ms. Ward said. "But look at how cute Mr. Winkle is!"

All of a sudden I gasped.

He had done it *again. He had done it again.*

As if being bumped by Mr. Winkle *one more time* weren't enough of a humiliation and a degrading experience in itself, it had to happen in front of thirty kids while I tried to talk about my great, wonderful, fulfilling career. Those who still clung to the thinnest faith that I was telling the truth returned to their desks and then tossed out a variety of boring questions like, "Did you go to college?" "Did you always want to be a writer?" and "How much do you make?"

I thought I was at least making some progress until I tactfully tried to avoid the last question by truthfully joking, "Less than half of any other male columnist," until the kid volleyed back with "Which is what?"

"Um, gosh, I don't know," I fumbled. "Less than Kenneth Lay, more than selling your plasma, how's that?"

"If you don't answer the question, we don't get extra credit," the kid said starkly.

"Oh," I said, nodding. "I get it."

"ASK ANOTHER QUESTION, MARK," Ms. Ward said harshly from the back of the classroom.

"Um, um, what's the worst part about your job?" Mark emitted with a tired sigh.

Suddenly, I perked up. "THAT is a great question," I replied. "That is a wonderful question! The worst part about my job is . . .

wow, I don't even know where to start! This is great!! Well, I get hate mail sometimes, that isn't too fun, there was this one time that I wrote in my column that Hanson was the suckiest band in the world and then an unbalanced thirty-two-year-old man threatened to come down to my office and shoot me in the head because Hanson was his *favorite* band. There aren't many more worthless ways of dying than that—jumping out of the log on Splash Mountain is one of them, I heard that a guy just did that. I mean, really, where did he expect to go? You don't just GET OUT on Splash Mountain. I was just there and I couldn't have successfully leapt off unless I was the stunt woman for *The Bionic Woman* and I had a trampoline at my feet. Or I was on LSD, but that's another story—anyway, don't get me wrong, Hanson totally sucks, sure, but I don't want to die for their suckiness in the only way that's dumber than getting mauled by a fake log on a Disney ride. Oh! I also have to deal with an idiot editor who, just because she gave birth to twins, suddenly believes that she knows everything, and keeps putting statistics into my humor column to make them more 'socially relevant,' but she fails to realize that the mention that 'Three thousand people died in drunk-driving accidents last year' is more of a buzzkill than a punch line, because let me tell you, an extra fetus does not a genius make! I mean, you guys are seventh graders and can you tell when a corpse is funny? *Hardly ever*, that's when!! And then, as you all saw, it's entirely possible that there are days when my column gets replaced by a dog dressed as a drone, even though he didn't go to college to be a drone, he didn't have a lifelong dream to be a drone, and word on the street has it that the reason he has to keep wearing costumes is because all of the fur on his back has fallen out due to shingles, because I asked around, I did. *I did.* I mean, no one tells you THAT in Journalism 101: 'Beware, a dog with a skin condition will steal your job.' Did you know that's not even a queen bee's outfit? It's not. Just an ordinary old worker bee. One in ten billion. And he takes my spot. MY spot. Ten years in this town writing that column, and a shitty little old diseased dog walks in and takes my spot, just like that!"

And then I snapped my fingers for emphasis.

"Wow," the kid replied, "you're the best guest speaker we've ever had!"

"Why, thank you," I replied, and I felt myself smiling again.

An avalanche of questions then came my way as the children begged me to tell them more about hate mail, death threats, people who died at Disneyland, LSD, and if I ever planned on throwing a poisoned steak over the fence of Mr. Winkle's backyard.

"Maybe not a poisoned steak, but I think I might toss a Hershey's Kiss or two." I laughed. "You can't tell me that little mutt doesn't at least deserve a case of the squirts after what he's done to me."

"Well, that's all the time we have for Miss Notaro on Career Day," Ms. Ward told the class, which was met with what sounded like a crowded baseball stadium sighing, "Awwwwwwww!"

It

was

glorious.

"Let's give her a round of applause for being so nice to come down here to talk to us," and then the class did just exactly that.

As the kids passed by me on their way out, I heard, "You rock, Miss Notaro!"

"You were better than body glitter, Miss Notaro," and "My mom says you have a dirty mouth. But I'm going to tell her you aren't any dirtier than my dad."

"Wow," I said to Ms. Ward when the classroom was cleared. "That went well, I think, don't you? That went so much better than I thought it would."

"Well, things have a tendency to pick up after profanity is used." She nodded with a tiny, little wicked grin. "It works better than sugar."

"Ooooooh, sorry." I winced.

"The luncheon for the Career Day speakers is in the teachers' lounge," Ms. Ward said. "So if you'd like a free sub and a can of generic soda, I'd love to have you come if you promise not to swear at our principal, although there's a PE teacher who's fair game."

"If she pants uncontrollably and the hair on her back has fallen out, you've got a deal," I volunteered.

Actually, after the last ten and only successful minutes of my Career Day talk, I was a little bit excited to go to the luncheon. I mean, really, those kids emitted sounds of grief when my talk was over, and finally, I felt as if I were on par with the other Career Day show-offs and their globes, alpha-hydroxy, cupcakes, and race cars. I could compete after all, even if I worked in an office where a two-pound, shingly fleabag outranked a columnist. I personally hoped that I would be sitting near the serial killer and the bomb-sniffing dog to inform them in general, passing conversation that even though I came empty-handed, relying on only myself and my trade to keep these tots entertained, I nearly brought thirty seventh graders to tears just by saying one word: "good-bye."

Ms. Ward and I grabbed two seats at one of several tables in the lounge, although the chiropractor and his carcass were nowhere to be seen and the bomb-sniffing dog wasn't even in a chair. Our table was occupied by a couple of teachers and their speakers, one of whom was a robust, jolly man in suspenders and the other was a woman who was so old that I could see right through her skin.

Just then, the principal stood up and cleared her throat.

"I want to welcome and thank you all for participating in our Career Day program," she said. "Before we get started with lunch, I would like to take some time for everyone to get acquainted with one another. So if our Career Day speakers would stand up and introduce themselves as we go around each table, we can get an idea of who all of our terrific speakers are."

So the rounds began; at each of the tables, a Career Day speaker stood up, told everyone his name and his job, and then sat back down. You could tell how impressed everyone else in the room was with each particular speaker's occupation: People smiled and nodded warmly at the fireman; people became stiff and unsmiling with the dentist, and people just absolutely looked away when confronted with an IRS employee.

Clearly—though unintentionally—we were being judged. It was

almost like the Miss America pageant, with each contestant having three seconds to strut his stuff and seduce the crowd, but without waxing, plucking, or liposuction, although from some of the reactions to the baker and the city council member, those extra efforts couldn't have hurt.

I also noticed that the reaction that each speaker got was not solely based on his occupation and jocularity alone; it also had a great deal to do with who went before you. The architect, on his own, probably would have scored fairly well, but being that he followed the noble, selfless researcher working on a cure for colon cancer, he might as well have been a circus clown.

Now, you would think that because of the unexpected though delayed spectacular response I got from my class, I really wouldn't have cared about winning this second round at Career Day, but you would be wrong. I was still flying pretty damn high from my "Miss Notaro Rocks" trip—so high, in fact, that I smiled at the IRS fellow. Frankly, I hadn't been that happy since I was planning my wedding. The joy I had found when realizing I had found a sucker to marry me was sharply overshadowed when the man I loved announced that he did not want to wear a tuxedo but would rather don a *salwa kamis*, the native dress of Pakistan. Despite my explanation that his comfort was truly not an issue at my wedding and that if my mother had to spend a lifetime looking at a photo in which he was dressed like a genie, her hate would be both endless and relentless, he still wouldn't agree to wear real pants.

That is, until the jubilant day that my mother told him, "Sure, you go ahead and wear that thing at the wedding, but if you do, you'd better plan on paying for the open bar, because, see, it's going to take a whole lot of Chardonnay, Bailey's, and strawberry margaritas for me and my friends to get over the fact that my eldest daughter is marrying a guy who showed up dressed like friggin' Barbara Eden."

It took the threat of a bar tab for two hundred people for my then boyfriend to agree to wear pants at his own wedding, but I couldn't have been happier.

And I hadn't been again until this moment; here I was, "my-groom-is-wearing-honest-to-God-pants" happy, and there was no way I was going to lose my buzz now. No way. I started to prepare for my turn and sized up the possible first acts at my table: I wasn't particularly concerned about the old woman, because honestly, what kind of workload could she feasibly handle when her high school classmates were now buried in the Valley of the Kings? I've handled tomatoes that were sturdier. At best, I concluded that she was either the bell ringer at a Salvation Army donation bucket or perhaps a crossing guard. Very noble indeed for a woman who probably had photos in which the Grim Reaper appeared by her side, but she was no Mr. Winkle.

No, I suspected that my Mr. Winkle was sitting across from me all bound up in his paisley suspenders and coordinating bow tie. This was my competition, I realized; this was the guy I had to look out for. From his ruddy cheeks and wire-rimmed glasses, I just had a feeling that I would have the good fortune of following Dr. Pediatric Heart Surgeon Specialist Guy who not only saved the lives of babies as a daily job, but spent his weekends and holidays traveling to Third World countries and Arkansas to operate on and cure impoverished infants and then fix a harelip or two with only moments to spare before catching the last helicopter ride back to civilization. He probably had a handwritten thank-you note from Mother Teresa hanging in his office signed, "Hugs, Mama T."

Damn it, I said under my breath, I just knew it. Frankly, I'd rather follow the cancer research guy than Dr. Baby Saver.

It was almost our table's turn to testify, and the anticipation was killing me.

"Come on, old lady, come on, old lady!" I chanted in my head as I mentally threw the dice. Then, as if on cue, the principal nodded toward the baby saver, signaling his turn to sassy himself down the catwalk.

He stood up, turning an even brighter flush of red than he already was, and proudly pronounced, "I'm Paul Wyatt, and I own several Burger King franchises in Chandler and Gilbert."

I almost burst out laughing. Not that owning Burger Kings was funny; I mean, if someone gave me a Burger King I wouldn't laugh, but I was shocked to see just how wrong I had been. So, so wrong. I breathed a massive sigh of relief and was ready to stand up for my turn when the principal nodded her head toward the human antique.

It took the old lady about a minute to stand up as her body unfurled into the shape of a question mark—a move that required the aid of two supporting teachers, I might add. Toss out the crossing guard, you'd need the posture of an exclamation point for that, or at the very least a semicolon, I smirked to myself silently. This one's a bell ringer.

Piece of cake. My chances were now good to excellent that I wouldn't have a very hard act to follow. No—my chances were now excellent to outstanding, that's what they were. OUTSTANDING.

Simply remarkable.

"My name is Frances Cross," the elderly lady warbled as she looked around the room and smiled the sweetest, most honest and appalling smile I had ever seen. "And I—"

"—am the one who makes you feel guilty for not dropping a quarter in my bucket after you've just bought yourself a big, fat Thanksgiving dinner at Safeway," a little voice in my head said, followed by peals of imaginary audience laughter. "Ring-a-ding-ding! Ring-a-ding-ding!"

"—and I," she continued in her wavery, delicate, little old lady voice as we all looked on, "was one of the first female pilots in World War Twooooooo!!!!!!!!!"

Twooooo, twoooooo, twooooo, I heard echoing all around me.

Oh my God.

Holy shit.

Sure. Of course. Well, *naturally.* It only made sense that when it was my turn, the doctor turned out to be a french fry hocker and the antiquity turned out to be nothing less than a NATIONAL TREASURE.

The laugh track inside my head stopped, replaced with thunderous applause, and I didn't understand until I looked up.

Looked up and saw the entire room not only beating their hands together for Frances Cross, War Hero, Feminist Leader, Archetypal Patriot, person who could donate herself to the Smithsonian *and they would take her*, but I saw the room get much, much taller. The room got the kind of tall when everyone else is giving Ms. Frances Cross, American Monument, *the lady you thought was a bell ringer*, a standing ovation and you are still sitting down because you are an absolute dip shit.

It was, indeed, simply remarkable.

There was only one thing I could do. I stood up, grabbed my purse, thanked God for not having any props to gather up, and made a move for it.

"Where are you going?" Ms. Ward said as she reached for my arm. "What are you doing?"

"Gonna get myself a bee outfit," I said simply, and headed for the door as rumbles of applause continued to hail from the skies.

Swimming with the Fishes

"Do you really want to wear that?" I said to Jamie as she came out of the bathroom of our hotel room. "I think it's too dressy. We're only going to Golden Gate Park."

"I would like to look nice for the Japanese Tea Garden," she replied, very matter-of-factly. "It's a very formal garden, and I've been wanting to go there since I was a kid. I want to dress appropriately."

"But we're on vacation," I said, motioning to her pleated wool skirt, her thick, cable-knit crew-neck sweater layered over a T-shirt, and a string of treasured pearls her parents had given her when she graduated from college. "You look like you're about to be knighted, or run for president of the Junior League. Put on some jeans. You'll be happy you did."

"You may be happy visiting the VERY FORMAL tea garden dressed as a mechanic," she replied, motioning to my overalls, "but you never know when you might run into a foreign Japanese dignitary, because I read in *Sunset* magazine that a lot of them visit this place. I don't want them to think that I'm the stereotypical crass American."

"You know, I really wouldn't worry about that if I were you," I volleyed. "The first President Bush fixed it for all of us because after yakking in the lap of the prime minister of Japan during a dinner, I'll bet a pair of overalls on an American girl wouldn't even get him to turn his head, unless I suppose I lunged at his fly while making a retching sound."

"Just how many days in a row have you worn those things, Gomer Pyle?" Jamie asked. "I checked your suitcase. You brought those, five T-shirts, and a toothbrush. You know, if Gap knew you were planning on wearing them every single day from solstice to solstice, they would have laminated them so we could have at least hosed you down."

"I am comfortable," I said adamantly. "I can move around, I have room to spare, and I just don't want another episode of the Spontaneous Corduroy Combustion, that's all."

"I'm sorry," Jamie immediately apologized as she lowered her head.

It was a sad day when that happened. Sad, sad day. Even thinking of it now almost kills me. I was on a weekend trip visiting Jamie in Marina del Rey, and I had packed economically so that I wouldn't have to check any bags on the flight over. That meant in my tiny little suitcase—which essentially can't be any bigger than a tampon box if you want to keep it with you—I had to pack economically. You could manage to squeeze a wider variety of wardrobe in your pack for climbing Mount Everest than you can in the dimensions of a suitcase the airlines deem as carry-on. I was basically able to bring a couple of pairs of underwear, a T-shirt or two, my pajamas, a stick of deodorant, and a little ball of dental floss because fitting in my toothbrush was nearly impossible. Now, this is where my favorite pair of brown corduroy pants came to the rescue, because they matched everything. Everything. And not only did they match everything, but those pants loved me so much that they expanded with me, and kept fitting me even when I got too fat for any of my other clothes. Plus, denying all rules of physics, they made my butt look deceptively smaller, almost like an optical illusion or fun- house mirror. My brown cords were my savior, my precious pet, my pride and joy. I loved them. I *loved* them. And because they matched everything so well, all I had to do was toss a couple of shirts next to the ball of dental floss and I had enough clothes for several days. I was a genius!

Unfortunately for me, Jamie and I headed to our favorite Mexican restaurant straight from the airport, where a large dollop of refried beans plopped right down on my leg, which sometimes happens with anxious eaters such as myself. I tried to wipe it off, but only succeeded in spreading the dollop into a large smear, simultaneously grinding the beans into the fabric of the cords as well. So, later that night, I changed into my pajamas, tossed my beloved brown cords into the industrial capacity washer and dryer in the laundry room of Jamie's apartment building, and they were good as new and ready for another day of wearing.

Oh, sure.

The next morning, I showered and got dressed, sliding into my brown cords, which, frankly, seemed a little tighter than usual, and looked even tighter. I was sure it was the industrial dryer that had made them shrink a little smaller than they normally did.

No problem, I thought, and looked around the bathroom to make sure that I had enough room for some deep knee bends, which, I've always found, can give you a little wiggle room if you do them right and stretch out your pants when you're in danger of popping up in a fashion magazine photo entitled "Big Mistake!" or "Think Again!" with your eyes blacked out.

And that's why I needed knee bends, my arms stretched out in front of me, bend one, nice and deep to get the maximum stretch potential, bend two, a little deeper just to get the ass compartment a little baggy, and right when I was in midbend on bend three, I heard it. A large, popped-bubble of sound, POP!!! like the crack of a baseball bat, loud and strong and quick. There I was, my knees bent, my ears ringing, and then I saw that millions of tiny, minute particles of brown fuzz had completely invaded the air around me, what looked like tiny brown flies were now silently floating slowly toward the ground as I automatically began swatting and blowing at them.

"WHAT WAS THAT?" I heard Jamie yell from the other side of the bathroom door. "Are you all right? That sounded like a rifle! You're okay, aren't you? Say something!"

"No, no, I'm okay," I said, finally standing up so I could open the bathroom door, and that's when I understood.

"Oh . . . my . . . God," I said slowly, not even remotely believing what I was seeing with my own eyes.

"Oh, Jesus, are you shot? Are you shot?" Jamie cried. "Open the door!"

"Oh . . . my . . . God," I repeated as the bathroom door swung open so Jamie could see.

She gasped and covered her mouth. "Oh . . . my . . . God! What happened?" she breathed.

"My pants exploded," I said as I shook my head. "My pants just . . . detonated. They . . . kind of . . . *blew up.*"

And then I showed Jamie how, just at mid-inner-thigh level, my pants had been pushed to the brink, and how, just at the inner seam, the pressure of my knee bends had cut through the fabric with the precision of a laser beam at a complete 360 degrees, slicing the pant leg off as if it were horizontally chopped by a guillotine. Not vertically, but horizontally, that's how much my gargantuan double-wide ass should NOT have been in those pants. They tore *against the grain.* The inner seam was still miraculously held together by several threads, although the remainder of the fabric that once bound the leg to the rest of my pants was now reduced to a brown thread cloud, some still floating in the air, some settling finally on the floor.

"Oh!" Jamie gasped again, covering her mouth. "Knee bends!!"

"Knee bends," I confirmed, aghast and nodding.

"It's amazing," my best friend offered. "It's as if they were cut by a knife. Right across. I've never seen anything like it! Or, for that matter, like that little brown haze behind you! Wow, look at that. It's the soul of your pants leaving its earthly prison."

"I thought those were flies," I confessed. "I was swatting at them, like a monkey. It turns out that my pants were not growing with me as I originally thought. It appears that my Chub Rub had simply worn away nearly all of the material of the inner thighs, giving me more room as they disintegrated further and further. Until, apparently, they could take no more. And they finally died of exhaustion."

"This is jaw-dropping," she marveled. "Those things were held together by nothing but dust mites! I've never seen the leg of a pair of pants simply shoot off before."

"It's just a miracle that this didn't happen in public, as I was trying on shoes or bending down to get taco shells at Safeway," I added. "But at least if I was home, I'd have something else to wear. Now I have nothing. Nothing!"

"You can wear something of mine until we buy you new pants," Jamie said, trying to solve the problem.

"You're a pear. I'm an apple," I reminded her. "This will never work."

"Even though you and Donald Duck are both apples, one of you still has to wear something on the bottom when you go outside," she proclaimed as she went to her closet and handed me a pair of pants with an elastic waistband, then added, "Please be gentle."

"Donald Duck always looked like a pear to me," I protested as I went back to the bathroom, peeled off my dead brown cords, and slipped on Jamie's pants.

"Are you kidding me? Look at that paunch, he is SO APPLE," she declared. "The Country Bears, those are pears; Eeyore, pear, Piglet, pear, but Winnie-the-Pooh and Donald Duck are of your kind, Johnny Apple Seat."

From there, we went to the Gap and I bought myself a nice big pair of farmer overalls with enough room to squeeze in an additional person in case I got that fat. And I have worn those overalls pretty much every day ever since, partially out of laziness, but mostly out of fear.

And I was reminding Jamie of precisely that in our hotel room after she cruelly called me Gomer Pyle.

"Listen," I said firmly. "Have you ever had your clothes explode while they were ON YOU? You don't know what it's like. The shock. The horror. The guilt. I mean, I DID THAT. I did that. I abused my pants to the point of *murder*. I can never have that happen again, do you see? Especially not on vacation when I have no other clothes. I just can't risk it. I can't."

"Well, that's true, I've never had my pants erupt on me, but I did hear the sonic boom it caused, remember? I thought we were being home invaded," Jamie said. "I'm sorry I called you Gomer Pyle. But I want to go to the gardens looking nice. So don't make fun of me. Okay?"

"Okay," I relented, and then whispered under my breath, "Aunt Bea."

We had an anxiety-filled taxi ride in which the cabbie, a relative newcomer to this country, had clearly watched too many reruns of *Starsky & Hutch* and/or *Dukes of Hazzard* on TNN and was applying excessive amounts of the things he was learning to his everyday life, such as attempting to fly in an automobile and driving on parts of the sidewalk people were already walking on. It was a white-knuckler of a trip, and as Jamie handed Njrjtishnmemim his tip, she gave him some to spare: "Just because I'd like to be buried in these clothes," she said with a pointed finger, "doesn't mean I want to die in them."

As we walked up to the entrance of the Japanese Tea Garden, it did look grand, indeed. Everything was manicured and perfect, breathtakingly beautiful. We paid our admission fee and entered the first portion of the garden, where we were met by a big sign that informed us immediately to USE CAUTION! We kind of shrugged, as neither of us sensed that we were in imminent danger, and continued up the path for several feet where there was a large, decorative wooden wheel about fifteen feet in height. The wheel did not turn, as it was stationary, and clearly was not intended for park guest interaction. It was just there to look at. Curiously, however, there was a woman on the top of it, who had *somehow* apparently scrambled up the side like a cat or a lizard, all in her three-inch heels, what looked like very expensive pants, a glittery halter top, and toting her Louis Vuitton satchel, rivaling Jamie for best dressed. Now, however, it appeared that she was stuck, as she stood at the top of the wheel and looked down while she shook her head at her husband or boyfriend, who was speaking to her very quietly, yet very firmly, in Japanese and motioning toward the ground.

"What is she doing up there?" I asked, trying to figure out how she even managed to scale the sides of it.

"Apparently not USING CAUTION." Jamie laughed. "Which she has obviously thrown to the wind! Cool. She's gonna fall, she's gonna get hurt, and we'll have something to laugh about *all day*!"

"If only she had used caution," I added with a giggle, "she could have avoided being the main attraction at the Tea Garden. They have some pretty good entertainment here for not even having monkeys!"

After standing and watching the lady continually shake her head and do nothing else for about five minutes, things got a little boring so we continued a little way down the path, where we were met again with another sign that emphasized, USE CAUTION!

"You know, is there a wall of fire, free-roaming crocodiles, or a lava pit that I'm missing here?" Jamie mentioned sarcastically. "I mean, we're on a path! The most dangerous thing that could happen is that I step in a freshly chewed wad of Bubble Yum."

"Yeah, as long as we're not scrambling up a giant wooden wheel like a squirrel in stilettos, I think we'll be okay," I added. "But just in case, Jamie, use caution!!"

"Hey!" she replied. "Don't distract me! I'm using my caution!"

We crossed a minuscule, minimalist concrete bridge—basically just a slab of rock—that spanned a tiny stream opening into a larger pond, a reflecting pool of sorts, where people were gathered watching the koi swim aimlessly about. It brought us directly behind the wooden wheel and the cat lady, who by now had captured the attention of people other than her husband.

"Use caution, Jamie, use caution!" I cried. "That fluttering leaf nearly impaled you!"

"Watch out for that boulder of a pebble someone has carelessly tossed in the path to harm us," Jamie warned me. "It must measure at least a quarter of an inch! Use caution!"

And then, just as I took my first step onto the second, small, minimalist concrete bridge, I saw it happen. As she walked slightly in front of me, Jamie took a step with her right foot, and as she picked up her left foot, I saw that Jamie was heading straight while the bridge curved.

"JAMIE!!!!" I screamed as loudly as I could. "USE CAUTION!!"

But it was too late. Way too late. Her left foot was already out over the water of the pond, and I watched it happen, as if she were walking over a cliff in slow motion. My best friend stared straight ahead and upward toward the wooden wheel, smiling pleasantly, her pearls gleaming, her skirt flowing, having no idea that she was a millisecond away from disappearing in a blur of wool pleats to swim with the koi fish in the much-deeper-than-it-looked reflecting pool.

I did the only thing I could do, which was reach out and grab her bra strap from behind, but as she went over, I heard my effort SNAP!! as I lost her to the water below.

It was a tremendous splash. That water just swallowed her whole.

She had not, in any way, used caution.

When she finally surfaced a moment later, I breathed a sigh of relief as she swam to the edge and began clawing at the muddy bank of the icky, murky, disgusting green pond, stumbling to get out.

"I fell into the pond," she said blankly as she crawled up over the rocks like a lobster. "I fell into the pond."

"I know," I said as I tried to help her up and maintain my composure and not to laugh as water rushed off her in torrents. "I told you to use caution! Didn't you hear me? I yelled it right as you stepped into the lake like a sleepwalker!"

"I fell into the pond," she said again, as she looked at me quizzically, her hair clinging to the side of her head in thick, wet strands that looked like seaweed.

I was amazed that there was any water left at all in that stinky, filthy pond because Jamie's fancy outfit, complete with her once-pretty heavy skirt and thick, wool-knit sweater, had absorbed water like a sponge. That was evident as it now drained off her like rain and created a puddle that was spreading quickly out beneath her and getting the whole path wet. Jamie was far more absorbent than we could have ever even imagined, kind of like a human tampon placed in a glass half full of pretty blue water. This water, however, was not a pretty blue, it was algae green, and made my soggy best friend smell like the Gorton's Fisherman.

I was trying to wring her out the best I could, but I was starting to lose my composure.

"At least we know you're not a witch," I said in between bursts of giggles, and trying to look on the bright side. "Or Jesus. You sank like a kitten in a bag of rocks! What do you have in your pockets, barbells?"

"I fell into the pond," she said again, still obviously stunned as I struggled to take off the wet sweater while leaving her T-shirt on and wrung out her sleeves. "The cat lady had me mesmerized. I was just going in for a better look. When I first fell in, I thought, well, this isn't so bad, I'm only in up to my knees, but momentum had me in its wicked, tight-fisted grip and I fell forward. Into the stinky piece of shit pond."

"It's okay," I said, as a flood of water rushed out of the bottom of her sweater as I squeezed it. "With a wire brush and a lot of Febreeze, we'll get that shrimping boat smell off of you! Eventually! Please tell me you didn't swallow any water! Stuck in the hotel bathroom with fishpond shits is the last way I know you wanted to spend your vacation!"

Just then, I heard Jamie yell.

"HEY!" She stepped forward and nearly knocked me down. "HEY, YOU!!"

When I looked up, I saw that something of a crowd had started to form; I mean, there were people who had seen Jamie walk into the pond and then crawl out, but now, there was a growing number of onlookers and they were staring at us.

But that wasn't all. One of them had a video camera. It was pointed at Jamie. And he was filming.

"WELL, GO RIGHT AHEAD!" Jamie roared at him as she stomped her foot and stretched out her dribbling arms. "GO RIGHT AHEAD! Get the whole thing! Did you get it all, huh? Did you get the whole thing on tape, you asshole?"

Then the Angry Little Mermaid took her shoe off and emptied out a whole Thirstbuster's worth of water. "Did you get that?" she bellowed at the video-camera man as she shook her shoe at him. "Did you get it? I hope you got it *all*! Sorry I didn't *drown* so that you could have something *really* good on tape!"

Frankly, I was rather hoping that because of this new development that people would think we were filming a movie, or perhaps that we were some young hopefuls handpicked to star in the remake of *Laverne & Shirley*, but I thought it was best to remove Jamie from the situation before she beat the man to death with one of her 160-pound waterlogged sleeves.

"Let's go to the bathroom," I suggested as I led her away, her watery shoes leaving a trail as they audibly squished with every step, leaking out a footprint.

"He was filming me!" she growled, *squish, squish, squish.* "That bastard filmed the whole thing!"

"Think of it as a compliment," I tried to reassure her. "Your incident was far more fascinating than the stupid lady stuck on top of the wheel. You had *action* going for you! You had drama! You had the element of surprise! Plus, I think I peed my pants laughing at you."

"You know damn well that we're going to see that footage pop up on some home video blooper show and he's going to win ," she said angrily, *squish, squish, squish.*

"Dude, I was basically naked at Disneyland after Splash Mountain and then evil children openly mocked me when I ate it in the dirt on Tom Sawyer Island," I told her, trying to be nice. "We'll do whatever you want for the rest of the day."

"Well, we could walk up to the Golden Gate Bridge and I could fall off that," she replied starkly, *squish, squish, squish.* "Or I could try to swim to Alcatraz. I really just want to go back to the hotel and take a shower. I smell like a California roll."

As we walked back toward the front gate, we passed by the wooden wheel, which was now empty and didn't show any signs of freshly spilled blood, and then we saw the first warning to USE CAUTION!, directly across from the ticket booth.

Jamie stopped suddenly, walked straight over to the booth, *squish, squish, squish,* and knocked on the window.

"Hey, in there!!!" Jamie shouted at the ticket lady, as a large droplet from my wet friend's hair plummeted to the ticket counter. "YOU NEED A BIGGER SIGN!"

Going Down

To be honest, I'd have to say I have a rather lengthy list of things I'd rather not experience on an airplane, and coming in in at least the top five would be hearing the terrified screams of other passengers.

Yet there they were, a small, collected grouping of gasps, cries, and screams coming from all directions.

I wanted nothing more than to join them, though I was too frozen to do anything but clutch my armrest.

It had been a horrible flight almost from takeoff; odd, loud noises emanated from above and below the cabin as we swerved our way into the sky, desperate to reach thirty thousand feet, and as soon as things appeared to be leveling off, we hit a trail of turbulence that was destined to bump us from state to state.

Things would calm down for a bit, if only to trick those of us seated in that airbus death trap that all was smooth sailing, and then, like a sucker punch, we'd hit another rumbling pocket of discord and passengers would begin another round of patiently holding their breath, trying to ride it out.

And that's exactly where we were when the terror struck—we were leveling out, just a minute bump here and there, when *WHOOSH*, all of a sudden the plane dropped suddenly and deeply, quickly and profoundly, as if we had fallen into a bottomless yawn in the sky.

Shrieks sprung up all around me; the gentleman behind me yelped like a dog. The pilot corrected the plummet immediately and straightened out, but in my mouth, I was still chewing on my heart, my stomach, perhaps even a tip of my small intestine. I had been far too stunned to do anything, I realized, during that moment in which it seemed as if God had reached down and hit the plane with a flick of a finger.

A minute later, my heart was still in my mouth, but I had started to breathe again.

That's when I looked down at the can of Diet Pepsi and thought to myself, Just what in shit's name are you doing? I mean, that plane had dropped, A LOT. It was the closest I had ever come to feeling a real, genuine smack of mortality. And if that's what it took to shake me back into reality, then so be it.

After all, my biggest fear (on land) was not that my husband would leave me for another woman or that I'd be imprisoned for a crime I didn't commit (but wanted to). No. My biggest, most tremendous, horrifying fear was that I would one day go on a diet, work night and day on the treadmill, bravely fend off the stabbing pains of hunger and luring pulls of temptation when I passed roughly 95 percent of all food housed on grocery store shelves, and, finally, after months and months of living gruesomely, depriving myself of every last joy and suppressing every human desire, I would be rewarded by reaching my high school weight, the elusive, holy grail of every woman on the face of the earth, and the same day that I stepped on that scale to reveal that triumph was indeed mine, that I had climbed the high school weight mountain and had beaten the odds, that I could, *yes*, fit into that pair of size six Jordache jeans and victory was my crown to adorn, the conquest mine to claim, the very next day I would get a walnut lodged in my throat and choke to death in a public place, or encounter a soccer mom driving her Ford Expedition while simultaneously making an appointment for an eyebrow pluck on her hands-free headset when she would sideswipe me and propel my nearly weightless, birdlike body out of my car, seventy-five feet into the air to certain death because she would be too busy trying to figure out how to get to her call-waiting without using her hands. That is my greatest fear, that I am skinny for only one day and I have spent the last months of my life hungry, sweaty, and with a headache.

What the hell was I doing with a Diet Pepsi when I had come so close to the brink of my own extinction? If this wasn't an example of how fragile, thin, and fleeting our opportunities to stay alive on this earth was, nothing was.

A Diet Pepsi?

For WHAT? To not consume 180 more calories in the last seconds of my life?

If I was going down, or if the opportunity was there and more than willing to present itself, as it very well just had, I was going to at least perish while drinking my favorite soft drink!

And then, just at the flight attendant walked past, I caught her arm and said, "Would you please bring me a glass of Pep—" but then I suddenly had a genius amendment to that thought and finished the sentence with the word "wine."

Wine, I thought to myself as I smiled and nodded as she walked away, *wine*. Why, yes, *wine*. Hadn't I deserved it? Hadn't I just about come that close? Because really, if we were indeed going down, if we indeed hit the next turbulence pit and did not recover and my run as a mortal had just crossed the finish line, then, yes, by all means, I should at least catch a buzz.

Absolutely! I chortled in my head as I seconded my own motion, bring on the wine!

It was a glorious glass of wine (to tell the truth, the attendant could have handed me a mug full of purple gas and I would have eagerly chugged it down) and quite precisely what I did indeed need. Gulp, gulp, gulp.

Within a matter of minutes, my nerves smoothed to the texture of velvet, my head had begun to clear the anxiety and I saw there was no reason to worry at all about being on a plane in a very bumpy sky. After all, I reasoned, we're in the same sky as clouds. Clouds like on the toilet paper commercial that I recalled may have featured something like a fluffy bear or angel bopping around from one soft cottony bank to the next.

That's right, I told myself, if this plane gets any bumpier, I'll just jump right out and sit on a cloud until this whole mess clears up.

And then I giggled.

I was drunk.

Drunk. Drunk off one glass of silly Chardonnay, drunk and giggly like a sorority girl who was having trouble holding on to not only her dignity, but her liquor as well. But add one glass of wine to one empty stomach and then multiply that by 30,000 feet, and well, you get sauced.

It was just shameful.

Certainly, hindsight is a glorious gift and a sharp, fine-honed learning tool when you have the benefit of distance, but that element was at least an hour's trip to sobriety or a cold shower away. In the meantime, there was mortification to be had, and I was rushing at it like a locomotive fueled by crystal meth.

Now, of course, getting drunk on an airplane because you are afraid the plane is going to crash is truly not a wise idea. In the first place, in the event that the plane does go down, the survival instinct inside all of us kind of counts on the fact that its owner won't be tanked when the moment arrives, since the use of all or a significant percentage of your faculties would be not only quite helpful, but rather relevant. Particularly, I might mention, if circumstances require that you have to go down the puffy yellow slide. Contrary to popular belief, the slide is not as simple and whimsical as it may initially appear. In fact, I believe it is in a sense complicated, despite the misconception that survivors, maimed and whole alike, simply step onto the slide and glide down it as if they were enjoying a day at the water park. The truth is disturbingly different. I have learned from a friend who once was employed as a flight attendant that the proper—and only—possible way to ascend the slide is to cross your arms and JUMP onto it. It's true. Watch the "Survival Tips for the Attentive" film the next time you're on an airplane and you'll see. There's no step, it's a jump. A quick, medium-grade hop. Now, I ask you, if I can't walk a straight line at this point, how is any inebriated passenger supposed to save herself with a complicated physical maneuver that pretty much requires the coordination and agility of Mary Lou Retton? Frankly, I do believe that the survival slide engineer should have added handrails for the benefit of those passengers who have been partaking of the hobby known as spirits, but apparently, no one had either the foresight to include them or ever considered that the alcoholics on the plane would stumble that far, a conspicuous and discriminatory act as far as I'm concerned.

It is at this point that it's relevant to mention that I'm drunk and sitting in first-class, thanks to my frequent-flier miles, and I'm in Row 1, seat A, otherwise known as "The Helper Seat."

The Helper Seat, for those of you who have not had the good fortune to sit in it, is the seat which, before take-off, the flight attendant is obligated to inform any passenger sitting there that "Since you're sitting in the first row, I have to ask you if you would assist me should I need some help. If not, I'll have to move you to another seat."

Now, in any given nine out of ten situations, I cannot help *myself*, let alone strangers, even when my judgment isn't riddled by substance abuse, so obviously, an answer escaped me. But I knew one thing for sure, and that's that I was determined to hang on to my first-class seat, and that I wasn't going back there. You know what I mean, *back there*, the poor part of the plane, where wine costs four bucks a glass, you get a Hot Pocket instead of a Caesar Salad with Grilled Chicken and Chocolate Mousse for dessert, and you're touching legs with a guy who has brought his own cocktail bar with him in a small Coleman cooler, no shit. The part of the plane that I am now unaccustomed to. I'm sorry, it's true. I have seen the promised land and there is no going back. My advice to anyone who has never sat in first class is simply, "Don't." Don't do it. *I mean it*. Compared with first class, everything else is just a rickshaw.

So, in light of that, I just nodded my head to the flight attendant before this plane even took off, signaling that yes, indeed, I will be your helper girl, although I was not exactly sure to what level of responsibility I had just committed myself. I mean, "help" is a pretty general term, don't you think? It could mean a lot of things. It could mean passing out peanuts; what if someone had an allergic reaction to peanuts? Clearly, this was not a peanut-free zone. I didn't even know CPR. I supposed I could fake it by punching people in the chest until the peanut popped out. Or now that we're in the Terrorism Age, it could have meant wrestling a passenger who's waving around a weapon—or a stupid asshole like Richard Reid who tried to light his shoe on fire—to the floor. Of course, *he'd* be in coach. He'd be stupid enough to be *back there*. That man was in coach and he tried to light his shoe on fire. *Anyone* who has ever flown on a plane knows you can't even *see* your feet when you're sitting in coach, let alone *put a match* to them. You're not even reacquainted with your feet until you're at the baggage carousel well after the plane lands. I believe the only person capable of touching his own feet in coach was a sixty-seven-year-old yogi whose main hobby was squeezing himself into mailing tubes used by architects, and even then it took him an hour and sixteen minutes to grasp his own little piggies on a flight from Albuquerque to Cleveland. But if there was someone as dumb as Richard Reid on board, guess who would be the one going down swinging? Me. It'd be me. The flight attendants wouldn't want to do that. I mean, of course they'd send out the new helper girl. "No one's emotionally attached to her yet and she weighs as much as all four of us!" That's what they'd say. So there I am, the helper, leaping onto the back of a terrorist like a feral cat while the flight attendants hide, all four of them together in the soda can cart. Or it could be a South American terrorist/guerrilla after money and I could be taken hostage. That happens to helpers, you know. They're helping, and all of a sudden, they're hog-tied and eating bugs in some jungle hut. Of course, I'd probably lose some weight, but then I'd gain it all back anyway when I got over the Post-Traumatic Stress "See, That's What You Get for Helping" Syndrome. Or I might achieve my ideal weight from starvation just to end up beheaded as an example to the other hostages. Sure, I'd be able to surpass my wildest dreams, and attain my *sixth-grade* weight, but how exactly is that positive if I am missing a head? Tabloids would call me the "Headless Hamburger Helper Girl," and the only guy who would get to see how much weight I lost would be the one sliding my cadaver into an oven like a baguette. And, if by any chance, the Hamburger Helper Girl survived, I bet the same day she was released she'd get squashed while scrambling like a golem to the first Cinnabon she saw, mowed down by a soccer mom with unruly eyebrows who was behind the wheel of a Ford Expedition.

So you see, in the event of a tragedy, not only have I done harm to myself, but I've put the whole plane in jeopardy because I forgot that I was the helper when I drank the wine, and seat 1A, just so you know, is their beacon of hope. Their very last chance. And that's just what I was pondering when I caught the flight attendant's arm and ordered my second glass of free wine, because, I figured, what the hell, I was drunk already, and well, impaired is . . . *impaired.* If I was going to lead people out the wrong safety exit on one drink, well, then I might as jolly well have another and perhaps even find some humor in it.

But you know, having two drinks sloshing around in an empty belly while you're on an airplane should come with this prediction: "Chances are likely to excellent that when you get up and stagger to the toilet-ette after downing your second complimentary alcoholic beverage, you will entirely forget to batten down the hatch that flashes the 'Occupied' sign outside the door and the pilot will walk in on you when you are in midpee."

In fact, I do believe it should be mandatory that the flight attendants pass on that nugget of knowledge when they are handing you that *numero dos* drink, as it certainly would have been helpful to me.

But there I was, and there was the pilot right after he opened that unlocked door and sucked the air right out of the powder room like a vacuum. It was an intimate moment, especially since I wasn't clothed from the waist down, but the sad fact is that an intimate moment can be too easily spoiled when one of the participants has a look of pure and absolute horror on his face. He looked at me, his mouth immediately dropped, his eyes grew wide, as if he truly did see a half-naked golem gumming a Cinnabon on the shitter.

Now, quickly, the very first thought that popped into my alcohol-soaked brain was, "Hey! No—wait wait wait—I mean HEY! Get back in your chair! *Get back there!* What are you doing over here, go fly that plane! Don't they give you guys bottles to wizz in or little straws to stick up there so that someone is in control most of the time? This isn't a radio-controlled aircraft! Go on, get *back there!*"

But instead, I smiled, waved, and said, "Hi!"

I said "hi." Complemented by a full-hand, frenetic, prom-queen wave, but really, tipsy or not, what are you going to say in that situation to wipe the disgust from the scene or even try to lend yourself a little shred of dignity? There's nothing. Absolutely nothing. All you can really do is suck it up and thank the good, righteous, heavenly Lord above that you didn't have a mound of toilet paper wrapped around your hand and were in a position of midhike.

Slam, the pilot shut the door hard and fast, although not quickly enough for the slack-jawed faces in seats 1C and 1D to get a load of the action going on in the poop booth.

Frankly, I didn't know what to do. Alone again in the potty, I thought about what happened and I guess it was too much for my currently handicapped thought process to handle because I began to laugh. I just laughed. And I kept on laughing until little tears popped out of my eyes and I found myself slapping my own, naked knee, to the delight, I'm sure, of my fellow first-class passengers, who undoubtedly heard my maniacal cackling because although the lavatory is self-contained, it is not a sound booth on a game show.

Finally, I pulled myself together, washed my hands, and opened the door, only to find the pilot still waiting on the other side.

He looked at me.

I looked at him.

He looked at me some more.

Say something, the voice inside my head commanded. *Say*

something witty, funny, say anything to make this whole thing seem not so bad as it really is.

All of a sudden, I had it.

"You know," I said with a little shake of the head and a wry, intentionally placed smirk, "I usually get paid for a show like that."

The pilot did not laugh. Neither did the flight attendant behind him or the spying little eyes from seats 1C and 1D.

"Really?" is all the pilot said.

"No!" I cried. "NO! I mean, no! You saw my legs and my fatty knees! Are you kidding? I was raised Catholic, my mom just came back from a Saint Francis pilgrimage in Italy and bought a huge statue to prove it, big as you. *Big as you.* Catholics aren't like that, they can be a little slutty sometimes, sure, and there's the pedophilia, but they're not allowed to be strippers! It's not allowed!"

And with that, the pilot slipped into the rest room and quickly closed the door.

And then locked it.

I went back to my seat, and when I looked over at 1C and 1D, they were still staring at me.

"I am not a stripper. I was a Catholic," I whispered to them, thinking inside my head that they should just mind their own business. After all, the guy who was supposed to be flying the plane was busy attending to his own needs, not the aircraft's. And, should some shit go down, it would be wise to have the Helper Girl on your side, lest she not find it in her wicked little inebriated heart to be vengeful enough to show you to the door without a slide.

Snakes

It was my husband who saw it first.

"Hey," he said, leaning toward the TV, "isn't that your old boyfriend?"

It's a question he asks me a lot, especially if he's watching *COPS* or *America's Most Wanted*.

"I told you, just because some guy on the news walks out of a trailer without a shirt on, has a beer in his hand, and is being questioned by the police doesn't mean I've dated him," I shouted from the kitchen.

"I think this is the guy who had the snake," he yelled back.

A thin shiver coiled up my spine. The snake. I even pretended that I liked the snake, named (I'm embarrassed to say this part) Sid Vicious, a thirteen-foot reticulated python that lived in a glass cage the size of a single-wide home, minus the do-it-yourself add-on.

Quickly, I learned to hate Sid, even though this was during the mid-eighties and boyfriends with snakes were just part of the deal. I understand the food chain and the order of nature, but actually witnessing a fat, sluggish reptile attack an ordinary field mouse was more than I could stomach. It very easily could be equated with the terrifying vision of *Vogue* and the former cast members of *Friends* joining together to declare a "Day Off from Anorexia" as models around the world descend upon their local Waffle Houses for the All-You-Can-Eat-and-Actually-Digest special.

I was especially horrified when Mary, a small white mouse I had named after the blind, pretty sister on *Little House on the Prairie,* was in the process of being digested. She had bravely managed to survive for nearly two weeks, hiding in a hollow knot of the tree branch that rested in Sid's cage. I really thought she was going to make it; she was very quick, and managed to roam freely about the cage without catching the snake's attention. I was devastated when she was eaten, my black, liquid eyeliner running down my cheeks.

"She went down in two bites," the boyfriend said as softly as he could. "Will you help me shave my head now?"

"This is just so totally sad," I persisted, sobbing.

"Man, I told you, you gotta quit naming them, dude," he said, nodding.

"I am so not a dude," I said, reminding him.

He kept nodding.

In the middle of summer, the boyfriend came home with thirteen rats in a box. "I'm gonna breed 'em," he insisted, and I just turned away as he placed all of them in an aquarium in the bedroom closet. That night, I had a nightmare that my mom was scratching at the window, and when I woke up, I realized that it was only the sound of the closet rats tearing up the newspaper in the aquarium, and made the boyfriend move them to the laundry room.

The next morning, I entered the kitchen just as the boyfriend was on his fifth trip to the trash can, holding a limp rat by the tail. "There's no vent in here!" he said, standing in front of the dryer and the steamed-up aquarium. "Six of them are dead!"

I looked at the remaining seven rats. "Ma and Pa are gone," I cried hysterically. "So are Carrie, Almanzo, and Mary II!" The boyfriend put the rats outside in the carport to give them some air, but then forgot about them after a meeting with his bong. By the time he remembered, the sun had shifted and had raised completely overhead, causing a magnifying-glass-and-ant type of scenario within the aquarium. I couldn't bring myself to look as Laura, Nellie, and Miss Beadle met the fate of their previously expired friends.

My hate was sealed and delivered one night as I was walking

down the dark hall and something batted me in the head and I saw something waving in midair, like the trunk of a circus elephant. I immediately flipped the light switch, and that's when I saw the first six feet of Sid, whipping around like a fire hose, mysteriously four feet off the ground. The snake had managed to escape from the cage, had squeezed through a tiny space in between the doorjamb and a bedroom door, and was now stuck. The boyfriend solved the problem by taking an ax and a crowbar to the doorjamb, trashing the dream of getting our security deposit back.

My aversion to reptiles of all sorts was duly confirmed several years later when a hippie suddenly put a four-foot iguana on my head one night at Long Wong's. My head quickly bowed under the seven-pound weight of the lizard, but when the hippie tried to remove his scaly pal, the iguana dug its claws into my scalp and refused to budge. For forty-five minutes, the hippie and three of my friends each took a leg and worked nonstop to get the lizard off, creating a slight commotion as thirty onlookers watched, including my then current boyfriend (the snake boyfriend and I broke up when he got married). Finally the animal pooped on my head and relaxed enough to release its claws, but I couldn't move my neck for a week and was forced to wash my hair repeatedly with liquid Tide.

I was thinking about that when my husband called again from the living room. "Hurry!" he shouted. "This guy on TV has a snake tattoo on his neck, too! It's got to be him!"

"What did he do?" I asked, coming into the living room just before the news segment ended.

"He won the Powerball," my husband said. "Are you going to leave me?"

"Even though I'm sure he's bought a triple-wide mobile home, a hydroponics system, and a big-screen TV by now," I assured him, "that thing on his neck wasn't a tattoo. It was moving all on its own."

"The front door to their trailer looked like someone had attacked it with an ax," my husband added.

"I bet it did," I answered, nearly hearing the sounds of another security deposit being kissed good-bye.

Babyless

"Nicholas," my sister said to my nephew over dinner several nights ago, "tell Aunt Laurie what you decided you wanted for your birthday."

"I can't," my five-year-old nephew replied as he sadly shook his head. "Grandma told me that Aunt Laurie doesn't love me enough to get me what I want."

"What?" I interjected. "What does Grandma know? She thinks that I was wearing white at my wedding! You just go on and tell me, you know I'll get you whatever you want."

"Really?" Nicholas said, suddenly perking up. "Well, then I want a first cousin!"

"Wow, I can't believe I'm actually about to say what I'm about to say," I said, completely stunned. "But Grandma's right."

I am, unfortunately, at that age.

I'm at the age when I meet girls I went to college with at the mall and they're pushing baby strollers while I'm pushing my credit card limit. At the age when my peers are planning for maternity leave and I'm planning to fake a pregnancy and a birth so I can have four months off. At the age when I run into friends in the checkout line at toy stores who are buying toys for their children and I'm buying *Planet of the Apes* action figures for myself. At the age when people—particularly family members—have no shame in asking, "When are you going to have kids? You guys better get busy!"

Frankly, that's a visual that I could really do without. I mean, the last thing that I want popping into my head when I'm sitting next to my Aunt Rita at a family picnic is a Technicolor picture of myself "getting busy." You try eating a hot dog *after that*. Besides, my title in our family is not "child bearer"; that's my youngest sister's role, which she has performed magnificently by producing two sons. My other sister is the "do-gooder," as she meets the challenges every day of educating children, and I am the "black sheep," a duty I have embraced enthusiastically; I have $3,789 of psychotherapy under my belt and a tragic credit rating to prove it.

Considering the above, I'm rather comfortable with my childless situation, but it apparently bothers other people. I can tell this as they wonder aloud about why I'm not burning up with baby fever, asking in whispers, "Doesn't your stuff work?," "Maybe if you ate less sugar," and my favorite, "There is a starving baby in China crying for its mommy, and that's YOU!" My mother is the one driving this bandwagon, despite the fact that it was her name that was signed on the bottom of the checks to both the psychotherapist and the collection agents.

I'm guessing that's the debt I'm expected to repay in the form of an episiotomy and Lamaze classes.

"It sure would be nice to have a granddaughter," I've heard her mumble as she cast a look in my direction.

"Write me a check for forty thousand dollars and I'll go to China and get one," I snapped.

"Don't be ridiculous," she replied. "You couldn't even pass a Spanish class in college, let alone talk to a baby in a language that doesn't have any letters!"

My mother will never understand why I joined the Babyless Club, checking my ovaries at the door and settling on a life without ever knowing what a belly button with an eight-inch circumference looks like.

The truth is that it was suggested at an early age and backed up with a second opinion during the psychotherapy years that perhaps my genes were not the best possible stock from which to spring progeny and carry forth the family lineage. It's a well-known fact that black sheep should never have lambs. You know what you get when you take a black sheep and give it a lamb? You get a thing called "supervised visitation," that's what.

I mean really, I'm just trying to be honest with myself. I've received several signs that I am not the sort of person who should be rearing young, feral or otherwise domesticated. The other day after I came home from the grocery store, I stood before my front door for several minutes straight, repeatedly pushing the car alarm device on my key chain, completely puzzled that my door wasn't opening while my car horn was blaring thirty feet from me.

The week before that, I felt the need to go number one, so I pulled down my pants and sat down, apparently unaware that I was sitting in my office chair. In my office. Thankfully, good sense shook me awake before I let the river run without the benefit of indoor plumbing beneath me, but for the rest of the day, I was frightened of my own special-ed potential, and kept myself in the house lest my bladder sound the alarm while I was gassing up the car, in the dressing room at Banana Republic, or making a deposit at the bank while simultaneously making a deposit on the floor.

And not too long before that, I was making dinner and searching in the pantry for tostada shells. Then, in a moment of brilliance, I said to myself, "I know! I'll do a search on Google for 'tostada shells' and that will tell me exactly where they are in the pantry!"

What would I do if I lost my baby at a Super Wal-Mart? Run to the computer department, pull up a Google screen, and type in "Where is the black sheep's lamb, and please don't anyone call CPS"?

And if that story still doesn't convince you, here's an honest-to-God true tale to try on for size: I was a little short of money a while back, and I will be perfectly up front and confess that I was getting ready to write Safeway a hot check. Sometimes, those things cannot be helped, especially if the Kenneth Cole Mary Jane shoes you have had a crush on for four months suddenly, and without warning, are marked off 30 percent. Which means if you buy three pairs, you *almost get the third pair free,* and I know this for a fact because I made sure to check in with my best friend Jamie, who uses math every day at her job as a microbiologist, so she has to be good at it.

I couldn't have been happier with my new pair of favorite Mary Janes in black, brown, and another backup emergency pair in black (listen, catastrophe happens—the next time you're wearing your favorite shoes and a sheet of vomit comes toward you, you'll wish you had an emergency backup pair, too) until I realized that my breakfast, lunch, dinner, and chocolate allowances for the next fourteen days were metaphorically sitting in my bedroom closet in three identical boxes. So yes, I spent our food money on shoes, but maybe if Safeway had a "buy two get one almost free" sale going on, the story might have ended a little differently.

So, needless to say, I was in a hurry to write my bad check to them and get out of there as fast as possible before someone noticed that I was wearing two weeks' worth of sustenance on my feet and had nothing in my checking account. The cashier told me the total, and I was fishing around in my purse, hoping to find a pen. This task, though simple, is not easy. My purse, as you might have suspected, is a bit of a black hole. I have always carried large purses, I have never been a tidy-small-purse gal who can only fit a lipstick tube and a house key into hers. Oh, no.

Not me. I have to have a purse large enough so that if Nazis were advancing into my village, I'd have enough room to shove half of my household belongings in there and a bunch of snacks for the trip. It's that big. I have a thing about being prepared, or at least having the accessories that make you *look* prepared. Not in the prepared sense that I have enough left over in my budget to buy food every week, but enough that if I were about to be taken prisoner, I would have no trouble finding ample room on my person to bring three pairs of Kenneth Cole shoes, a twelve-pack of Nutty HoHo's, and perhaps a toothbrush with me.

And in addition to being large, my purse has a lot of stuff in it already, so it therefore acts like a filthy washing machine, in a sense, with objects churning against other objects, which leaves everything with a brown, aged, and somewhat germy patina. My husband, in fact, will not stick his hand in my purse, not to get the car keys or even cipher money because he claims that his hand comes away with tobaccolike flakes under his fingernails and adhered to his cuticles, despite the fact that I quit smoking three years ago and have changed purses six times since then. He calls the residue Insta-Grime; I just call it "urban purse compost."

All of these factors were now complicating my search for the one writing instrument I knew I had in my purse. But finally, somehow, my fingers felt it—a ballpoint pen with the cap still attached, so I grabbed it and whipped it out of my purse with the ferocity of victory.

Now, unfortunately for me, the pen did not come out alone. In fact, it had a friend with it. A friend named Tampax Deodorant Extra-Extra-Extra Super Size, a friend who had, due to the washing machine effect in my purse, come free of its confines, had escaped from its pink plastic applicator prison, had busted through the plastic wrapper, and had its tail, or rather its string, caught neatly in between the body of the pen and the pen cap.

And, as I whipped the pen out of my purse, the companion tampon came with it. Since its escape it had grown, had fully blossomed to the size of a badminton birdie, its once white and cottony surface now dirty, brown, and mottled with Insta-Grime. The simple, generic, and unlikely action of whipping the pen out of my purse gave the tampon enough of a G-force, gave it a shot of condensed momentum, administered a punch of concentrated energy so forceful that it launched out of my purse in an upward arc on a heartier and faster trip than light or sound has ever taken. Now, given the gift of flight, my dirty, nasty tampon vaulted up and over the ATM terminal of the checkout counter, high and proud, slicing through the air, *Matrix*-like, *WHOOMP WHOOMP WHOOMP*, end over end as its little gray cotton tail whipped wildly about behind it.

Six eyes watched the spectacle unfolding before them—the pair that belonged to me, the pair that belonged to the cashier, and the pair that belonged to the bag boy who I had, for quite some time, suspected took the short bus to school or was just a really nice kid, or, as I have established previously, possibly Canadian. Transfixed, horrified, oddly drawn to the liberation of rocket tampon, we were simply unable to tear any of those six eyes away. They trailed the dirty cotton comet as it continued to sail over the counter, hit the wall behind it without a sound, and then dropped to the floor, where it bounced a couple of times before it finally rolled to a stop.

As the other four eyes looked at my two, nobody said a word.

Not a word.

Oh Jesus, I thought to myself as I wrote out that bad check in record time, please don't let the Canadian delayed kid start playing with my visually revolting feminine hygiene product while I'm still standing here, please God.

I grabbed my groceries and ran out of that store like I had shoplifted a big hunk of expensive cheese or something, leaving my cotton stopper behind like the deserter it was.

I never looked back.

And that is why I should never have kids. That is why. Because my mom never lobbed a sullied Tampax grenade over the checkout stand at the A&P, and I'll make a fair bet that your mom never did, either. People who cannot control tampons can't possibly control children. If my mom had ever performed a magic tampon trick like that in my presence when I was a child, I would have turned out a whole lot weirder than I am already, so that's a lot. I mean, who knows, it could have led to something as drastic in my adult life as listing my occupation as "bead artist," making my own spirulina pills, or burning incense on a regular, perhaps even daily, basis. *Not good.*

And I wasn't alone, either. Most of my closest friends had also committed to a childless existence, and a good percentage of them weren't even forced to by a judge in a court mandate. We took our cue from my courageous friend Meg, who had decided even before she finished grad school that kids were not for her and her equally revolutionary husband, Bill.

"I want to go on vacation when I want to, I want nice furniture, and I like sleeping for longer than two-hour intervals," she said. "Babies are not for us. Don't get us wrong, we love babies, babies are wonderful. We just prefer them at a distance." Meg, I thought, had a point; so thought a bunch of our other friends. The rest of our lives were gonna be great; my friends and I would be able to vacation together for the rest of eternity, talk on the phone for as long as we wanted without tiny voices interrupting, and we could encourage one another to blow half a month's worth of food money on shoes because we would never have to look into the hungry eyes of our kids.

Our lives would rock. We were in the Babyless Club.

Besides, I've been close enough to the fire to know that I don't necessarily need to step into it. As I mentioned, my sister has two kids, and honestly, I've seen what they've done to her. The CD she has in the player of her car is the ubiquitous *Dino Rap*, of which she knows all the words and began unconsciously singing at a recent family dinner: "Velicor Raptor is mean/he hisses and growls/one swipe of his claw/will surely disembowel." Physically, she can't stay up past 9 P.M. and actually confessed to me that her eight hours a day at work was her "private time." Her private time? I thought to myself. What the hell is going on in that house? Yes, I've seen my five-year-old nephew burst into a round of inconsolable tears when the cheese slid off his pizza, in her hallway there is a spot that was once the debut of an abstract doody mural created by a self-absorbed two-year-old, earlier this week the same two-year-old woke her up before dawn to pull a booger out of his nose, but can it be so bad that work is a sanctuary? Her *private time*?

Obviously, my friends had no such privilege, because one by one, they began to defect. Sure, there were some that I knew didn't stand a chance against a Bellini sleigh crib with a coordinating suite set or an Eastertime window display at Baby Gap—I mean, nothing can make a woman ovulate faster than a smocked dress in pastel colors. It is nothing less than an arrow right through your ovaries. Some of my friends were easy baby prey. My friend Jeff and his wife, Kristin, for example, went in search of a Vornado fan and simply wound up on the wrong aisle at Target, finding themselves face-to-face with an Eddie Bauer car seat and, *bing*! within seven days he gleefully proclaimed over the phone to me that "his boys could swim!"

And then he giggled.

I just sat there for a minute, trying to decode his message. My boys can swim, my boys can swim. Hmmm. I didn't know. I didn't have the faintest idea. Anagram? My scab is my own? My icy-ass womb? I'm sown by my sac? My icy snob swam? Cow Man, by Missy? None of those made sense. Maybe it was a male thing, I decided.

"Hang on," I said before I covered the mouthpiece and beckoned to my husband. "Jeff said, 'My boys can swim.' "

My husband stopped dead in his tracks and his face dropped. "They're having a baby?" he asked in a voice that sounded like someone had swung a bag of russet potatoes into his gut.

I rolled my eyes. "Jesus, you are such an idiot," I said, returning to the phone, and that's when I heard Jeff yell, "We're having a baby!"

Jeff was my first friend to become a parent. It was an odd transition for all of us. As long as Kristin was only pregnant, I could ignore the fact that my best friend's life was going to change for good, and that nothing would be quite the same again. But I wasn't prepared at all. Then, when the baby showed up, things turned wild.

"Oh, you should see him!" Jeff bragged. "The doctor says we have to wean him soon, but he's the best suckler the doctor has ever seen. He just latches onto Kristin like a vacuum cleaner. He's in the ninety-ninth percentile of sucklers!"

I was aghast. I hadn't heard such talk since the last time I drank margaritas and dialed a 1-900 number. Suckling, weaning, latching! Who wanted to know that kind of stuff? I certainly didn't. Nor did I want the visual accompaniment of a topless Kristin, now a MOTHER, holding a baby with a mouth that had the properties of a Dustbuster.

Months later, my friend Amy was the next one to drop out of the Babyless Club, and the last time I talked to her, a hard-nosed, take-no-shit investigative reporter who has toppled administrations and exposed scandals from high to low, told me (and I quote): "Trying to pick up some freelance work so I can buy the $140 Petunia Pickle Bottom Toddler Tote I've been lusting after."

Now, honestly, really and truly, it's not as if I resented my friends' sojourn into baby land, whether or not they had broken the childless oath. I was actually happy for them—now Amy could shop at Baby Gap, where a baby arrow once had not only knicked her ovaries, but pierced her uterus as well. And for a couple of months, I get to be the thinner friend. Babies are adorable and I love looking at pictures. But when Jeff declined to come to my first-ever book signing because his four-month-old son was invited to a party at the railroad park with a bouncy house and a face painter, I finally got it.

My friends didn't just have babies. They were parents.

I was now Beta and everyone was leaving me for VHS. It's true. Over the last two years, I've lost more friends to babies than I did to booze. One by one, they'll call, drop the bombshell over lunch, or break the news with, "Actually, I can meet you for happy hour, but I can't drink. So don't force me to. And I can't tell you why. So don't force me to. Okay, I'm pregnant. I'm not supposed to tell anyone yet, so if my husband asks you, you forced me to, okay?"

And that's when I know I've just become obsolete to my mommy-to-be friend—that's when I know I'm outdated, last year's model. We've got about six to eight months of friendship time left, and then we go our separate ways.

"Congratulations," I'll say. "It was nice knowing you."

In fact, I've taken to performing a new ritual when I get baby news: I smoke a cigarette, say a bunch of curse words, and then pour out a beer for my homies who have passed to the other side, because they're gone. It's a proven, scientific fact that once someone has a baby, there's only a one in 125 chance that she'll ever answer the phone again when you call. It's an activity that she's relinquished along with watching a movie with a higher than G rating, driving a sedan, and eating meals in any joint that doesn't serve chicken nuggets.

It's like the series *Left Behind*—and if you think battling the devil during Armageddon sucks, try being left behind in my world and getting someone to go with you to a party on Friday night who's not only going to bring along a third wheel, but that third wheel's Aprica stroller, vibrating bouncy chair, and floor carnival and can only stay until said third wheel throws up or shits his pants.

Finally, suffering loss after loss, the Babyless Club had shrunk down to me, Jamie, and its founder, Meg, while Jeff unabashedly, and occasionally in public, demonstrated dances from *The Wiggles*, Amy slung a well-earned Petunia Pickle Bottom Toddler Tote over her shoulder, and when I heard her newborn cry, I had to warn my friend Colleen that if she suddenly started whipping her boobs out all over the place, I was cutting my baby visit short and wouldn't be coming back until baby Ben's bar mitzvah.

"We should have had more gay couples in our club," Jamie said, exasperated. "All of a sudden, we've become the satellite station out in space that you see in horror movies. 'They're all gone, Captain, well almost. The only thing left behind is some green slime, an abundance of chocolate calcium chews, and three wrinkled old broads who shriek when you pull out a onesie.' Not only are we childless, we're on the friggin' Baby Ghost Ship."

Then, one day not long after that, I got the impossible phone call.

"I need to talk to you," Meg urged. "I have news."

"Congratulations," I replied, shaking my head. "It was nice knowing you. I'm guessing it was a Bellini Elegante four-drawer chest with changing-table top in the mahogany finish along with the Vanessa crib. Who could resist? I heard my uterus sob when I saw it in Amy's nursery."

"Nope," I heard Meg say. "Moses basket, Pottery Barn Kids, pink gingham."

"Wow," I replied, stunned. "That's an unfair fight. That's a sucker punch."

"Do you think three hundred dollars is too much to pay for it? I mean, it really is just basically a big breadbasket," she stumbled, "with eyelet ruffles and pink gingham! PINK GINGHAM!"

"Well—" I started to reply.

"Well, of course it's worth it!" Meg said, answering her own question. "Especially if we use it for the second one."

"The . . . *second one?*" I gasped.

I hung up immediately and called Jamie.

"I know just what to get you for your birthday," I cried when she answered the phone. "How's about a nice hysterectomy?"

An American (Drug-Smuggling) Girl

"I'm," I proclaimed loudly and proudly to the man who had a gun secured at his hip, "an AMERICAN!!!"

My mouth was dry, my hands were shaking, and I was scared out of my mind, especially now that the border agent was glaring at me and obviously pretty pissed.

Still standing in Mexico, wishing desperately that I could just fly the five feet to the United States, I realized that I was probably the shittiest drug smuggler of all time.

I totally sucked, but it wasn't my fault.

Merely two weeks before, I went to Walgreen's to pick up a prescription for allergy medication and discovered, much to my horror, that the pharmacist wanted eighty dollars from me, which was sixty dollars more than what I paid the previous month.

Now, you know, if I'm going to spend eighty bucks on drugs, I'd better have to show ID and sign my name for the release of a controlled substance. I'd better be walking away with some Vicadin or her delightful little cousin Xanax in my little paper bag, not a month's supply of Allegra, which you can mix with alcohol *and nothing happens.*

In my book, that's called "a one-trick-pony drug."

"You have got to be kidding me," I said as I stared at the white lab coat. "I paid less than that to have my gallbladder removed, I got knocked out for that, I got to keep the bedpan *and* a box of tissues. When did sneezing become so expensive?"

"Since Claritin went over-the-counter, the manufacturer of this drug raised its price, and your insurance company decided to make it a third-tier drug, which means it's 'lifestyle enhancing,' and not a necessity, like Viagra," the pharmacist informed me sympathetically.

"Wow, how appropriate," I replied. "The activity of breathing is now considered less important than giving an eighty-year-old a boner. You know, if Allegra was oil, the marines would have invaded and we'd have bombed the manufacturing plant by now."

So when I went home and told my husband that ounce per ounce, Allegra was worth more than cocaine, we decided to stage a standoff. A Mexican standoff.

After all, isn't that one of the perks of living in Arizona, the land where you can die in fifteen minutes of dehydration during the summer if skin cancer doesn't kill you off first? But the trade-off is that cheap tequila and pills that we can actually afford are a mere border hop away. Now, I had heard from about a million different people who had all gone to Mexico and come back with all sorts of things—big, giant bottles of Valium, cigarette carton–size boxes of muscle relaxers, antibiotics, you name it— and it was there for the taking. They came back from a Mexican pharmaceutical shopping spree like they were Liza Minelli the weekend before she was due to check herself into a joint called "Resurrections."

We'll go to Bisbee for a couple of days, we decided, hang out, then swing by Nogales on the way home, grab some lunch and pick up our stash. It was a plan.

It was a bad plan.

After our trip to Bisbee, we pulled into Nogales, and let's just say for the interest of those who have not been there, border towns aren't exactly known for their glitz and glamour. Suddenly, I felt like I was on a soundstage and at any minute, a grainy image of Benicio Del Toro in cowboy boots was going to cross the street in front of me and Catherine Zeta-Jones would turn the corner with a big, creepy cocaine clown in her hand. And mind you, I was still on the American side of things.

We parked our car on the Arizona side, paid five bucks to an old man who looked like he'd sat in that dusty, dry parking lot for so long he'd simply mummified, since essentially all he could move were his eyes.

Now, getting into Mexico is easy, because Mexico knows you're not going to stay. I mean, who really wants to fill out a change-of-address form sporting a zip code south of the border, unless you've just killed your pregnant wife on Christmas Eve, assaulted your scalp with a box of Feria frosting, grown a jaunty goatee, and lost your chubby-hubby pounds to do your best "No, I'm not the guy who killed his pregnant wife on Christmas Eve, I am Ben Affleck, hombre!" act? Who really wants to stay there long enough to see if Mexico has seasons? Vincente Fox isn't putting on airs, he knows the score, he doesn't need to shell out extra pesos for any sort of border patrol. Instead, there's just a turnstile. Getting into the Target by my house is harder once you consider the metal detectors.

We went through the turnstile and we were in.

Within five minutes, I had the goods—enough for almost a whole year, plus some other bonus things I picked up as long as I was there—swinging from my hands in a plastic bag. I was so happy. I was jubilant. I now had the ability to breathe out of one, possibly both nostrils, and for about the same price that my insurance company wanted to charge me for two months' worth.

"I'm a little hungry, do you want to get something to eat?" my husband said.

I scoffed. "Are you kidding?" I said, taking in my surroundings. "I feel like I'm in a United Way commercial. I just saw *a donkey*. To be frank, I really enjoy my intestines in their present, parasite-free condition. Sure, I'd like to lose some weight, but a tapeworm is the last way I'd like to do it, except becoming a prisoner of war. If you have to boil the water here just to drink it, there's no way I'm touching taco meat."

Ready to go home, we walked to the U.S. border checkpoint, which isn't as loose and loving as Mexico's. At all. It's easier to get backstage at a State of the Union address than it is to get back into your country. My husband and I stood in line with the other people ready to be questioned, scrutinized, and searched, and it was just about our turn when I saw it: a sign in black and white that proclaimed that IT IS THE LAW THAT ALL PHARMACEUTICALS AND MEDICATIONS PURCHASED IN MEXICO AND BROUGHT INTO THE UNITED STATES MUST BE ACCOMPANIED BY A VALID U.S. PRESCRIPTION.

I looked at my husband in a panic. He looked at me, then looked at the plastic bag hanging from my wrist.

I had a prescription. I did. It was just two hundred miles away at Walgreen's.

"Back to Mexico!" I hissed quickly. "Back to Mexico! Go back to Mexico!!"

We bolted out of line and walk/ran back to the marketplace, where we found a seat on a bench and sat.

"What are you going to do?" my husband said. "Do you think the pharmacy will give you your money back?"

I openly laughed. "Not even with a pretty *por favor*," I replied. "I'm stuck. I'm totally stuck. There's only one thing left to do."

My husband looked at me.

"Smuggle," I said, shrugging. "It really isn't breaking the law. I have a prescription. If this goes to trial, I'm sure Walgreen's would bring it down to the courthouse. It's either that or try to find a toy manufacturer to get the Allegra compressed and formed into the shape of a clown doll."

"Oh my God," my husband said, shaking his head in disbelief. "Oh my God. Please tell me you're not going to stick a year's worth of Allegra up your ass."

"Wish I could, but with my luck, they'd probably shoot out as bullets. No, they're going into my other black hole," I said as I opened my purse and started shoveling in my purchases. "I've just spent two hundred dollars on this stuff, there's no way I'm leaving it on this bench and walking away."

Back at the border checkpoint, we bravely took our place in line again, and this time, I noticed the cameras all around and above us, which had, without a doubt—in jerky, fuzzy black-and-white Circle

K burglary footage—captured our previous appearance in line as we stood for a while, chatted, made fun of the people in front of us, the plastic bag swinging in my hand, then as we suddenly noticed the horrible, horrible sign, reacted with the appropriate melodrama, ran out of line, and then returned five minutes later with no sign of the plastic bag, save for my bulging and gaping open purse, me looking as if I were Winona Ryder on a shopping spree or conducting research for a role.

When it was our turn, the border agent motioned us over to his station.

Deep breath, I told myself as we walked to his counter, be cool. Be cool. Stay calm. Act casual. *Do not* act like a smuggler.

"Citizenship?" the border agent, a gruff, surly, stocky, and sweaty man, said.

Be cool, I reminded myself.

I stepped forward, my arm outstretched, my driver's license in hand.

"I'm an *American*!" I proclaimed excitedly, as if I were auditioning for a public service announcement boycotting any products manufactured by the axis of evil. Or France.

The agent looked at me drolly and glanced at my license. "You with her?" he asked my husband, who nodded. "Citizenship?"

"I, as well, am an American, sir," my husband said so subserviently that had I not looked at him out of the corner of my eye, I could have sworn he was standing at a full salute.

"What were you doing in Mexico?" the border agent asked as he looked at us with suspicious, angry eyes.

"We ate lunch, sir," my husband, the fake marine, lied.

"You came all the way down from Phoenix to eat lunch in Nogales?" the agent questioned, raising his perspiration-dotted brow. "I don't believe that."

This was the precise moment that the stuttering began.

"No. Ub—ub—ub—ub," my husband, whose face had now turned the color of a hot tamale, said. "Bisbee! We were in Bisbee for the weekend!"

"Bisbee," I added, nodding vigorously. "Bisbee!"

"Did you buy anything while you were in Mexico?" the border agent asked, his eyes narrowing in on me.

I looked back at him, smiled as best I could as my face flushed with hot, hot fear, nodding and shaking my head at the same time, giving him more of a convulsion than an answer.

He gave up on me and went to his subordinate little puppet, the fake marine.

"Did you purchase anything while in Mexico?" he asked my husband.

"Wa—wa—wa—well, *I* didn't," my husband, the man I am joined with for life, the man whose underwear I wash, the man who just sold me up the lazy river without so much as a fingernail being tugged upon by a pair of border patrol pliers, answered, and then looked at me from the corner of his eye.

"And what did you buy?" the agent said, putting both hands on the counter and leaning toward me. "Did you buy pharmaceuticals?"

I paused for a moment. "Y-y-yes," I whispered, lowering my eyes as my hands started to shake.

"I know you did," the agent replied, smiling a very fake smile, I might add. "Empty your purse, please."

So I hauled out the booty with my sweaty hands, spread it all out as the agent looked on, shaking his head.

"Is this all for you?" he asked me.

"Yes," I nodded as he pointed to one of the boxes. "That's for my allergies. And that, that, that is for my asthma. That one is for my back pain. Those are for—um—for—uh, *lady troubles*, and those are because I get these really bad headaches that start on one side of my head and then work their way over to the other side but then eventually I always just end up throwing up anyway."

When I was done spouting off my medical history, I realized I was an eighty-year-old woman from Palm Beach.

"When I asked you if you bought anything, why did you lie?" the agent asked me harshly, clearly very irritated, and it was at this point that I thought he wasn't a border patrol agent after all, but a sales rep from Merck totally pissed off that I had cut him out of his commission.

But I didn't know what to say, and I was so scared I gave him another convulsion, the only thing I had not purchased medication for.

"When you are asked a question, *especially here*," he said to me quite sternly, "it's in your best interest to tell me the truth! Do you understand?"

"I do," I answered simply as he glared at me, and I had the feeling that I had just lost two hundred dollars and I was going to be talking to a judge very soon. Apparently, I had also taught everyone in line behind me a valuable lesson as they began taking all of their purchases from the *farmacia* out of their purses and fanny packs.

I was convinced that I was going to jail, and I even toyed with the idea of asking the guard if I could take one of my pills before he arrested me because I had a definite feeling I had a throw-up headache charging my way.

I looked at my husband again, and his face was so flushed he looked like he had just had a chemical peel. He had a little mustache of see-through beads gathered on his upper lip, and he was moments away from watching his wife get cuffed as a drug mule trying to run antihistamines, an inhaler, and one little pink pill because she was just too damn impatient to wait the week it took for Monistat 7 to really work, across the border.

"What can I say?" I imagined myself addressing a jury of my peers. "I want to breathe, I hate to sneeze, and if any one of you has ever been itchy down there, well, you know you would have done the same thing."

And then, against all odds in favor of a miracle at this particular moment, another guard came over to the station and nodded to the guard that was hating me.

"You wanna go on break now?" he asked my mean guard.

"Yeah," my guard said, wiping his brow with his sleeve, then gave me one last dirty look, and simply walked away.

He walked away. Just left us standing there, with all of my medication, enough drugs on that table to start my own rest home. Then the other guard followed him, leaving us alone at the counter.

And that's when I opened my purse, swiped my drugs into it, and very, very, *very* quickly walked away as fast as I could without generating electricity between my thighs.

The narc that I'm married to followed behind by a couple of steps, and when we finally reached the car and got in, neither of us said a word until we were at least ten miles outside of the Nogales city limits.

"We are assholes," my husband finally said, still visibly shaken. "I can't believe we did that. That was horrible! I never thought we'd get out of there. I'm so glad to be out of there!"

"Yeah," I agreed. "No thanks to you, Donnie Brasco! 'No, no, I didn't buy anything. Nope. Not *me*. Not *I*.' Stoolie!"

"Stoolie?" my husband shot back. "What about you and your 'I'm an *American*!' act? Are you aware that you said it in *a Texas accent*? 'Ahm ehn Ah-meh-rih-cahn!!' Oh! Oh! And 'This is for my LADY TROUBLES!' *Lady troubles?* Where *are you*, Charleston, South Carolina, circa 1940?"

"No, I was in MEXICO, about to go to PRISON!" I shouted.

"But yer ehn Ah-meh-rih-cahn!!" my husband shouted. "Who's on more medication than my grandma!"

"You are a dork," I said matter-of-factly.

"No, you are a dork," he retorted. "And you are never going to Mexico again."

"I already know that," I informed him.

"And we are never telling anyone about this, okay? No one. No one needs to know what idiots we are. Okay?" he said firmly.

"Okay," I agreed.

"Swear?" he insisted.

"On Ah-meh-rih-cuh!" I swore.

Burn the Mother Down

What is he doing? I asked myself as I stared at my supervisor, his mouth flapping, his hands flying furiously about as if he were a mime or presenting a liturgical dance.

There he was, giving me my walking papers by demonstrating my nonnegotiable departure with a series of complex yet mystifying gestures of some sort. I came to the conclusion that he had either choreographed a hand movement symphony entitled "Your Position Is Being Eliminated," or he had woefully mistaken my stubbornness for hearing impairment.

"So you see," he said, his spastic, hyperactive arms finally coming to a stop, his palms out facing toward me, "we cannot approve your request for a leave of absence for your book tour. You'll have to terminate your employment here if you wish to go."

"But—" I said.

"We only grant leave of absences for extraordinary circumstances or business-related events, and your book tour does not fit within one of those requirements," he continued.

"But—" I tried again.

"And additionally, your column for the website will be canceled as of August first. From then on, your job title will be an HTML editor and you'll post pages on the website," he said.

"BUT," I said loudly, and using my Angry Jazz Hands move to catch his attention and show him that he wasn't the only one who could impersonate a synchronized swimmer from the waist up, "I'm not asking you to pay me for the leave of absence, the book tour is indeed business related, I happen to find it extraordinary, AND I have no idea how to post web pages."

"Well," my supervisor said with a Grinch-like smile that ate up his entire face, "you'll have to make some decisions then, won't you?"

And with that, he got up and walked out of my office. I had been booted out of my job, just like that. No explanation, no reasons, just out. It was like I had been banished from a TV reality show, except there were no dramatic close-ups and no one hugged me.

I didn't want to quit my job, I really didn't. But since the Mr. Winkle incident that woefully exposed exactly what my bosses thought of me, things hadn't exactly been smooth sailing behind the door of my little office. I had suspected when the higher-ups stopped saying hello to me and ignored my salutations that I was figuratively leaving the Tower of London and heading downstairs to meet a guy in a mask. I will admit I am not a quiet little worker bee, as evidenced in the E-mail the Editor Escapade, which I had a feeling had a great deal to do with what just happened. I am a loudmouth girl, it's totally true, I can't possibly deny that. But I did my job, I was proud of the work I had done, and, frankly, I was hired exactly because I was a loudmouth girl.

When the Grinch left my office, my head was spinning. I had just been fired, but without the benefit of my beloved severance. They were going to make me quit.

Mystified as to what my next move should be, I naturally made the wrong one.

I called my mother.

"Oh God," she said sharply and slowly. "I knew it. I just knew it. Are you asking to move back home? Because if you are, I certainly can't turn you away, but I will tell you that you will be sharing your old room with my new Hepa filter humidifier/aromatherapy tower, my collection of Suzanne Somers's ThighMasters, my mini pipe organ, your sister's collection of Beanie Babies, my wall cabinet of

Diamonique, and the new meat preserver I just got. Did I tell you that with this thing you can keep ham for two years?"

"YES, YOU DID," I replied. "And P.S. Mom, *anyone* can keep ham for two years, *anyone*. It's just a toss-up of which family member you're going to con into eating it. My sisters and I made a pact that we will no longer eat any carnivorous products at your home if we haven't brought it over ourselves, because unless we take that precaution, unless we protect one another, one day I'll be eating a pork chop and you'll tap me on the shoulder and say, 'Good, huh? It's good, right? You know I've had that thing hanging in a closet since 1998?' "

"Now that you're out of a job, you should be welcoming air-vacuumed meat on your plate," she informed me. "I just can't believe those bastards won't let you go on that book tour. You have to go. You've worked your whole life for this. And you're *old*, unless you're Moses or a Styrofoam cup. What sons of friggin' bitches."

I gasped. You could have stuck that meat preserver vacuum hose right into my lungs and the air could not have been knocked out any faster than from the shock I had just experienced. I was *shocked*. I was really stunned. My mother—and I may have entirely misinterpreted the situation due to my emotional duress, I'll grant anybody that—sounded supportive.

"Wow, Mom," I said quietly. "You really understood that?"

"Of course I understood it," she snapped. "I'm your mother. I also know you stole painkillers from my prescription bottle when I had my root canal in 1982. I know everything."

"I'm sorry," I squeaked. "But they were Percodans."

"Oh, we're even," she said. "I borrowed some of your Vicadin when you had those kidney stones so I could sleep on the plane ride to my pilgrimage."

"You went on a holy quest loaded?"

"I don't like to fly over big bodies of water, I can't swim. What, you think Saint Francis could have stopped the plane from going down?" she questioned. "He's a nice saint, sure, but he's not Jesus. He doesn't have that kind of power! Now listen, being that I'm your mother and I know you, I will also tell you that every time you leave a place, you burn that bridge. You're like the Nazis, you have bridges burning all over the place. You're whole résumé is on fire. This time, take it easy, just in case you need them for a reference later on."

I knew my mother was only looking out for me, but she was wrong. Some of my bridges had burned, that was true, and I would not argue that the e-mail campaign was probably the equivalent of bringing a gas can to this bridge, but I was seldom the one who detonated the dynamite. Sometimes, I've even been *on the bridge* when it went down. I've been fired, laid off, eliminated, whatever, *seven times*. That's not me burning bridges; if you ask me, there's a stalker arsonist with my picture taped to his bedroom wall. Besides, in this case, if I couldn't even get a flimsy, made-up answer about why I was losing my job, I was pretty sure a reference was out of the question.

Technically, I also think that burning the bridge involves storming out in a hotter-than-hot moment, screaming the appropriate equivalent to "Kiss my grits!" and making a physical gesture enacting that very phrase. I faced several obstacles when contemplating this avenue; for one, I had accumulated far too much desk and office accessory decoration—I now had the entire cast of the *Planet of the Apes* action figures proudly displayed: Dr. Zira, Cornelius, Dr. Zaius, General Ursus, Gorilla Sergeant, Gorilla Soldier; a whole cast of farm animals that pooped root beer–flavored and chocolate jelly beans; a pair of Farty Pants; and a Homies diorama complete with a prison bus, the sum of which made a quick, clean get-away nearly impossible unless my car was a U-Haul. The second factor was the realization that, as an adult with a mortgage and digital cable bill due every month, the days of getting fired up and telling my SOB boss to take my job and shove it were indeed long gone. The complications of securing insurance, rolling over your retirement account, and figuring how to get the most out of your remaining vacation and sick days had squashed the quit-on-the-spot maneuver for almost everyone, not just me. Once you move out of retail and fast food, that scenario barely exists anymore unless you're a member of the adult entertainment trade, and even there you have to consider the loss of free STD tests.

After college, the procedure of quitting resembles a military maneuver, and "kiss my grits" is replaced with a mad dash to schedule appointments to get your boobs and asshole fondled, examined, and squished so that at least you can be confident you're abandoning your health insurance while hopefully cancer free, since the phrase "preexisting condition" has now become the most chilling term known to man. And you think you're doing the right thing by embarking on the medical version of the Full Service Car Wash, you think you're doing the responsible thing.

And I did think that I was doing the right thing when on the suggestion of several people at work and because he was the only doctor left on our dental plan that didn't operate on a rent-to-own-your-own-teeth basis, I called Dr. Bill to get a routine dental checkup to fix any problems.

Now, please pay attention to this part, because this is a lesson that took me six appointments and a whole lot of oral mutilation to learn. If you want to buy pot from a guy named Dr. Bill, or Dr. Don, or Dr. Ted, or get him to set up your hyponics garden, or hire him to DJ a party, that's fine. That is cool. Call him for that. But never, never, *never* give anyone who has coupled the "Dr." title with a first name and turned it into a "handle" access to a body part when he has the equipment to render you senseless with happy gas, lest you pick up on the fact that he has absolutely no idea of what he is doing and is indeed running amuck with scrapers, sharp tools, and drills at his disposal.

In your mouth.

Drilling into your head.

Okay, now, yes, I did indeed book an appointment with Dr. Bill, who I was thrilled to discover was the only dentist left in this country who still actively engaged in the use of nitrous oxide because really, this could have been my last chance. I was too old to go to raves and none of my friends still had a job with open access to canisters of whipping cream, so it was something of a last hurrah.

However, once I was under, Dr. Bill began talking me into obscene things. Before I knew it, he picked up a hand mirror and invited me to gaze at his handiwork, which I agreed to, mainly because I was pretty high and would have even sat and stared at another airing of *Mother, May I Sleep with Danger?* if given the opportunity.

I took the mirror into my own hand, took a gander, and nearly, very nearly passed out. He had drilled so deep into my tooth that I swear I saw indications of sunlight shining through from my nostril. It was so deep that there was barely any tooth left at all. I think there were bats hanging around up there.

"What are you doing in my tooth, mining for diamonds?" I asked as a puddle of drool slipped down my chin.

"Hey, do you feel it?" he asked.

I shook my head no.

"Then no problem!" he said with a Dr. Bill laugh. "Big cavity, breathe deeper. I'm putting porcelain fillings in, they'll look like real teeth!"

That's good, I thought to myself, especially since you've drilled away so much of the enamel that each molar looks like a little tiny teacup. There was so much room available now that I could have stored nuts and grain in each of them for the upcoming winter.

"I heard those porcelain fillings cause a lot of sensitivity," I begged off. A good friend of mine had them, also coincidentally installed by Dr. Bill, and she said she would have less danger in her mouth when eating if he had implanted Soviet-produced mines.

Dr. Bill stopped his drilling, looked me square in the mask, and said, "What kind of fillings do you want? The old, cheap silver fillings that will poison you eventually and make you crazy, or the ones I would give my wife? Which ones do you want?"

Little did I know at that point that it may have helped clarify the situation if I had asked Dr. Bill how he felt about his lovely *esposa*, Mrs. Dr. Bill.

I truly believe that he had probably just found out that Mrs. Dr. Bill was fooling around with all of his dentists friends, because porcelain fillings were the equivalent of miniature lightning rods that attracted massive thunderclaps of excruciating pain, mainly when anything came near them, including my tongue. I found this out the hard way when my mouth finally sobered up later that afternoon and I tried to do something flagrant, silly, and careless like drink some water. As soon as the liquid got even remotely close to the filling, a jolt of resounding pain that was not unsimilar to sticking your nipple into an active electrical socket shot up through my head like I had been golfing in a rainstorm. It was like having a camel suddenly and swiftly kick you in your privates, but only if your privates were located in your mouth.

The next week, when I returned to Dr. Bill's, I was determined to protest any further nerve damage in my mouth. He hooked me up to the tank before I even sat down, got me high, then did the other side while I was off floating into another dimension, listening to his E-Z radio station and thinking that Eddie Grant was never delivered the accolades of genius that he was due with his masterpiece, "Electric Avenue." When Dr. Bill was done that day, he had completely ensured that I would never eat anything other than 75-degree food and stuff from Hometown Buffet that didn't require mastication.

On my last trip to Dr. Bill, the unthinkable happened. Sure, he had rendered me chewless, but what happened that day is nearly unspeakable. It's honestly off the map of horror.

There I was, being high in the chair, when Dr. Bill finished and then handed me the mirror again. This time, I knew better.

I shook my head vigorously; the last vision of the well he had drilled in my tooth was still haunting me at night when I slept, and I kept having nightmares that volcanoes were erupting out of my jaw. The last thing I needed to see this time was an exposed sinus or the bottom part of my eyeball.

"No, thank you," I said politely.

"Oh, come on, it's pretty," he said, "Go ahead. I think you'll like it."

If this clown tooth-painted on me I will shit, I thought to myself, expecting to see a daisy or a butterfly reflecting back in the mirror image. But I didn't. What I saw terrified me even more.

"What is that?" I asked, pointing to the mirror image of my molar. "What did you do?"

Dr. Bill beamed proudly.

"It's gold," he nearly giggled. "It's a gold tooth!"

"Oh," I said slowly, the mirror falling into my lap, "my God. Oh my God. You gave me *a gold tooth*? I have a gold tooth?"

"Pretty, isn't it?" He grinned.

"Pretty?" I ripped my nose mask off. "Who do you think I am, Biggie Smalls? Come on, a gold tooth? This is great. I am now legally qualified to pursue a profession as a pimp! If I ever go to the Philippines and yawn in public, I will be dead within thirty seconds and someone will find me in a dirty old gutter with rusty pliers hanging out of my mouth."

"But it sparkles when you smile," Dr. Bill informed me.

"Do I look like a Sonic drive-through to you?" I asked. "I don't need a light show in my mouth. I just want to use up my insurance and then be able to chew. Do you know that I eat like a snake now? I have to swallow things whole!"

This just turned out great, I thought, soon I'll be unemployed, I can only eat things that have been whipped, pureed, or can be dissolved by saliva, I now have a gold tooth, and I'm going to have to join someone's posse.

While fending off my hunger pains due to my inability to eat adult food, I slowly began relocating my office to my house, box by box, grocery bag by grocery bag. I'd carefully pack the poop jelly beans in between my files and my books. My supervisor, the Grinch, would come in every now and then, stand at the doorway, and say, "Have you made a decision?"

"Nope," I'd answer.

I got my boobs mammogrammed and spent the next several days with the little pins taped to my bull's-eyes because I decided to keep them to play a "look at my new piercings" joke on my husband, but he never noticed and I was finally forced to remove them when they got fuzzy and linty and eventually made my boobs look like an onion bialy. I got my Pap smear done, had some moles removed, and tried to talk my doctor into some butt liposuction as long as I was there, but he just kind of looked at me with the expression that said, "Please. I just ate lunch."

I was almost ready to go.

I just didn't know where.

Sure, I was going on my book tour, but after those few weeks were up, I didn't have the slightest idea of what to do, and I was all too aware that my book would come out, and very, very possibly sputter, fail, and that would be it. The book had gotten almost no coverage, not even from my own newspaper, which meant no one would even know about it. I had the searing review from *Kirkus* that did me no favors, and a sinking, sinking feeling.

I had no prospects, I had no offers, just the all-too-real understanding that the little I had in savings wasn't going to get us very far, and if we lived like college kids, it could stretch maybe a couple of months. Maybe I could pick up some freelance work here and there, I thought, and maybe I could get a job as a cashier someplace until I made some more contacts and got some steady brochure, pamphlet, and kitchen-gadget-review work. Things looked bleak. Quite bleak, in fact, but they didn't look much better if I stayed and was relegated to the position of web page poster, which I had never done in my life. It was clear to me that my bosses figured that the combination of moving me to a job that I had no business being in and also taking away what I loved to do was the right mixture to make me walk away. And they were right.

And I was scared shitless.

In all honesty, I knew that I really wouldn't be able to stand myself if I blew off the book tour and stayed in a horrible job that would get worse week by week.

I told myself I could figure it all out when I got back.

The day that I packed Dr. Zira and Cornelius was one of the last in my office with a door. Everything that wasn't directly visible—hard copies of my columns, pens, notes, all of my work—was already gone, all of my drawers were empty. It was the day my book came out. Nothing revelatory happened, my world didn't shake, didn't even tremble. I took another box out to my car when I left for the day.

"Did you make a decision yet?" the Grinch said as he stood in my doorway.

"Nope," I answered.

I was packing my Homies and the prison bus diorama about a week later when I heard my e-mail bell go off and it was my good friend Theresa.

"Something's going on," her e-mail said. "Your sales rank on Barnes and Noble.com just jumped fourteen thousand places to three hundred."

My e-mail rang again. It was my agent, Jenny, from New York.

"Barnes and Noble picked *Idiot Girls* for one of their top summer reads. This rocks!" she wrote.

I checked the Barnes & Noble website.

Idiot Girls was at 300.

Theresa and I were checking it frantically every fifteen minutes. That's a lie. I checked it every minute. I kept printing out the pages. I couldn't believe it was real.

An hour later, it was at 212.

An hour later, it was at 173.

An hour later, it was at 13.

The phone rang. It was my editor, Bruce, who had warned me previously not to get caught up in the obsessive-compulsive cycle of checking my ranking every fifteen minutes because it was destructive, addictive, and wasn't really representative of anything except for my neurotic tendencies and that particular hour before the rankings were updated again.

"Oh my God, oh my God, are you seeing this?" I asked him, barely able to retain my inside voice and actively engaging in my Dork Dance in my almost empty office. "We're number thirteen on Barnes and Noble. I can't believe it! Are you seeing this? Go to the page right now!! WE are number thirteen. I know you told me not to read into these things, but we're only going to be thirteen for about three more minutes, so just play along, okay? Be number thirteen with me!"

"No, you're right, I don't care about being number thirteen on Barnes and Nobles for three more minutes," Bruce said sharply. "But what I *do* care about is that *Idiot Girls* is number twelve on the *New York Times* bestseller list next week."

Everything went quiet. Everything stood still. It was so, so quiet. Amazingly quiet.

"*Mother trucker,*" I finally said.

It was the only thing I could say.

Then I called my husband, I called my mom, I talked to my dad, who was sure it was due to the placement he had advised next to the *Auto Trader.*

And then, I sat back in my chair in my almost empty office, and I cried.

I bribed a coworker with a Milky Way bar to go and tell the Grinch.

He came by my office a couple of minutes later, and stood in the doorway.

"Congratulations," he said with his Grinchy smile. "Have you made a decision yet?"

"Nope," I replied.

Another Big Cheese in the department e-mailed that afternoon and asked if he could send out the news in a company-wide memo.

"Of course," I wrote back. "Just as long as you include the part about how you are canceling my column in a matter of days and making me an HTML web page poster instead."

He did not include my suggestion in his memo.

In a couple of days, when I was sure that I had packed up everything that meant anything to me—the Homies, the *Planet of the Apes* figures, the Pull My Finger Fred doll, and my Farty Pants—I turned the light off in my office and closed the door.

I looked back once. I loved that office.

I went home, packed a bunch of things into a suitcase, and wrote a letter. The next morning, I put the suitcase by the door and sent my letter, via e-mail, to the Grinch. I would have liked to deliver it myself in his preferred method of communication, sign language, maybe throw in a light show by my opening and closing my mouth a couple of times really fast, and truly, truly, *truly* bring the phrase "Kiss my grits" to life in a performance unparalleled in any other workplace in the history of man, but what can you do.

I called my letter "Guess What? I Made a Decision."

That bridge burned like it was *made* of dynamite.

Then I took a taxi to the airport and when I got there, I boarded a plane to go on my book tour, and left for New York.

Acknowledgments

Thank You . . .

Bruce Tracy, for being the incredible editor that he is and letting me go full-tilt boogie with this book. I am amazingly fortunate to have him as an editor and a friend, and I truly cherish that, as well as for the opportunity to teach him just what and who a Chupacabra and Otis Campbell are.

Jenny Bent, for not laughing when I tripped over a curb in the East Village, stumbled about fifteen feet, and then landed flat on my belly with a loud HUMPH!!! If that doesn't show your love, nothing does, JB. I know it took a lot to hold it in. Thanks for everything.

My family; Curtis, my UPS guy; Hugo and Allan, my mailmen; and anyone else who has to put up with me on a daily basis.

Nana, who lets me say horrible, filthy curse words in front of her and just pretends to be deaf and not hear them. I love my Nana.

Jamie, for still being my best friend after thirty years, and to my other best friend, Jeff, despite his sad little attempts at three-way calling. Just so you know, we hate it when you do that. Please get a better phone; yours sucks.

The sweet, kind, and patient Annie Klein, for sticking by me still; the darling and irresistible Adam Korn, for letting me talk his ear off; and the charming and delightful Mickey Rolfe, for always, always, always making me laugh.

Kelly Kulchak, Shari Smiley, Kathy White, and Sonya Rosenfeld, for still accepting my phone calls and for working with me. You guys kick ass. Thanks also to David Dunton; Nina Graybill; Pamela Cannon; Beth Pearson; Amelia Zalcman; Dan who makes the book covers; Kimberly Obitz; Meg Halverson; Bill Hummel; Theresa Cano; Kathy Murillo; Doug Kinne; Katie Zug; Sessalee Hensley; Jules Herbert; Donna Passanante; Craig Browning; Duane Neff; Amy

Silverman; Deborah Susser; Cindy Dasch; Sonda Andersson-Pappan; Beth Kawasaki; Eric Searleman; Charlie Levy; Patrick Sedillo; Charlie Pabst; Becky, Marie, and Rhonda from Fairfax; Bill Homuth; Sharon Hise; Leigh, Jeff, Val, and everbody else from Metro; the Public Library Association; the Arizona Library Association; bookstores big, bookstores not so big, and bookstores little, for being so kind when I come in and start scribbling in your stock; and, absolutely without a doubt, the girls Nikki, Sara, Kate, Sandra, and Krysti.

And the biggest thanks to all of the Idiot Girls out there who took the time to e-mail me, join the club, submit their Idiot Girl story to the clubhouse, come to a reading, or read through the books, nodding their heads because they *knew*. Thank you, from the bottom of my soggy little rotten-tomato heart, and I so totally mean that. You make me so proud to be an Idiot Girl because you undoubtedly prove I am in excellent company. Rock on, my sisters. We shall rule the world one day.

Love,
Laurie N.

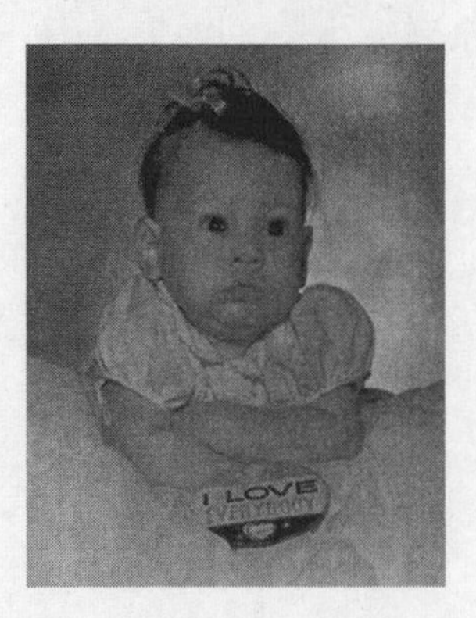

Laurie Notaro is currently unemployed and childless and enjoys spending her days searching for Bigfoot documentaries on the Discovery Channel, delights in a good peach cobbler, and has sadly discovered that compulsively lying on her headgear chart in the seventh grade has come around to bite her in the ass. Despite several escape attempts, she still lives in Phoenix, Arizona, where she is technologically unable to set up the voice mail on her cell phone, which she has never charged, anyway.